STORMY SKIES

For Judith, who has stuck with me through thick and thin

Stormy Skies
Airlines in Crisis

PAUL CLARK

ASHGATE

Published by
Ashgate Publishing Limited   Ashgate Publishing Company
Wey Court East   Suite 420
Union Road   101 Cherry Street
Farnham   Burlington
Surrey, GU9 7PT   VT 05401-4405
England   USA

www.ashgate.com

British Library Cataloguing in Publication Data
Clark, Paul, 1954-
  Stormy skies : airlines in crisis.
  1. Aeronautics, Commercial. 2. Airlines--Management.
  3. Financial crises.
  I. Title
  387.7'068-dc22

  ISBN: 978-0-7546-7887-8 (hbk)
         978-0-7546-9756-5 (ebk)

Library of Congress Cataloging-in-Publication Data
Clark, Paul, 1954-
  Stormy skies : airlines in crisis / by Paul Clark.
      p. cm.
  Includes index.
  ISBN 978-0-7546-7887-8 (hardback) -- ISBN 978-0-7546-9756-5 (ebook)
  1. Airlines. 2. Airlines--Customer services. I. Title.
  HE9761.1.C55 2010
  387.7--dc22

                                                            2010020874

Mixed Sources
Product group from well-managed
forests and other controlled sources
www.fsc.org Cert no. SA-COC-1565
© 1996 Forest Stewardship Council

Printed and bound in Great Britain by
MPG Books Group, UK

Contents

List of Figures

Note on Chapter Titles

The chapter titles are derived from song titles recorded by The Beatles.

'I Should Have Known Better'
From the album *A Hard Day's Night*, Parlophone, released 10 July 1964.

'Tomorrow Never Knows'
From the album *Revolver*, Parlophone, released 5 August 1966.

'Love Me Do'
Single, Parlophone, released 5 October 1962.

'I Want To Hold Your Hand'
Single, Parlophone, released 29 November 1963.

'You Never Give Me Your Money'
From the album *Abbey Road*, Apple, released 26 September 1969.

'With A Little Help from My Friends'
From the album *Sergeant Pepper's Lonely Hearts Club Band*, Parlophone, released 1 June 1967.

'Strawberry Fields Forever'
Single, Parlophone, released 17 February 1967.

'Here Comes the Sun'
From the album *Abbey Road*, Apple, released 26 September 1969.

All songs were written by John Lennon and Paul McCartney, except 'Here Comes the Sun', which was written by George Harrison.

Acknowledgements

I must thank my old friend and colleague Stephen Shaw for suggesting that I tackle the task of writing this book. To be perfectly frank, I was not particularly keen to take it on at first, as I could already imagine the anguish of slipped deadlines and lost family weekends. So it is with pleasure, mixed with relief, that I can now thank Guy Loft, Carolyn Court, Margaret Younger, Gillian Steadman and all the editorial and production staff at Ashgate Publishing for the amazing patience and kindness shown to their lazy author. Happily, the days when I would freeze in terror and guilt when an e-mail from Guy appeared in my Inbox are now in the past. I also thank Linda Cayford for her proofreading skills. Linda's eagle eyes and helpful suggestions are much appreciated.

The ideas and opinions in this book are not mine alone. I have been fortunate in persuading a small army of industry figures to share their own views. They are Jim Barlow of Sabre, Christi Day of Southwest Airlines, Professor Peter Belobaba of MIT, Richard Dyer of Friends of the Earth, Professor David Keith of the University of Calgary, Paul Finklestein of Pratt & Whitney, Manique Gunasekera of Sri Lankan Airlines, Tim Jeans of Monarch Airlines, Patrick Bianquis of Air France, Hubert Horan, Professor Robert Essenhigh of the Ohio State University, Tony Tyler of Cathay Pacific Airways, Patricio Jaramillo of LAN Airlines, Paul Griffiths of Dubai World Airports and Randy Tinseth of Boeing. To all of them I say, 'Thank you'.

Often, discussions with contributors only took place thanks to the patience and generosity of assistants and secretaries, who were unfailingly courteous to me. I am grateful to Nancy St Pierre, Susanna Fernandes, Karine Delrieu, Kitty Cheung, Thomas Brabant and Sherry Nebel.

Several organisations have given permission for material under their control to be reproduced. I would like to thank John Pritchard of Worldmapper, whose cartograms reproduced in Chapter 7 are both original and thought-provoking, as well as Brett Serjeantson of MediaMiser, Lisa Marsala of Interbrand, Mary Pat Clark of the Pew Research Center for the People and the Press, and Jason McGeown of Maplecroft who kindly allowed the reproduction of research data.

I would especially like to mention Alan H. Hess of Hess Travel, who penned the exquisite comedy sketch about revenue management and gave permission for it to be quoted in Chapter 5, and musician Dave Carroll, who generously found time during a busy touring schedule to recount the full story behind *United Breaks Guitars*.

In addition, I have called upon former colleagues and lifelong friends for their contributions. They are Louis Busuttil, Daniel Sallier, Philippe Fonta and Christian Scherer of Airbus, Nico Buchholz of Lufthansa and Captain Chris Schroeder of Qatar Airways.

There is another ingredient necessary to sustain an author through dark days of frustration, doubt and despair. Close friends have rallied round and, despite being spread around the globe, have always been on hand to offer encouragement and a metaphorical couch. I am grateful to Anaïs Marzo-Costa, Patricia Bausor, Erin Egan-Mesny and Katia Tripod for encouragement and laughter.

Lastly, and most of all, I thank Judith, Christopher and Robin for their faith in me. Life was hard during the period when this book was written but, when I needed them most, they were always there to keep me going.

Preface

I am old enough to remember every major airline economic crisis since the jet age. This is not a boast, nor is it something that I particularly wish to celebrate, as my confession is merely a disturbing reminder of the ever-quickening passage of time. But I have witnessed history repeating itself time and time again. The temptation to write about the most recent airline crisis, which can be traced back to the autumn of 2008 and has lasted well into 2010, was thus very strong.

In describing this book, I need first to say what it is not. *Stormy Skies* is not a compendium of startling new business models or processes offering an antidote to the ills of the crisis. Neither is it a blow-by-blow account of the downfall of the many airlines that have collapsed. That would be too depressing and serve no useful purpose. Rather, the book aims, through a series of essays, to shine a light on key commercial challenges that the airline industry is confronting. I offer no guarantees that airline executives who decide to apply any of my ideas, or those of my contributors, will emerge from the next downturn unscathed. However, I do believe that the subjects addressed in *Stormy Skies* are highly relevant to today's airline business environment and should not be overlooked.

As I have no affiliation with any airline, aircraft manufacturer, airport, supplier, user group or industry regulator, I have felt free to express my views in an objective way. This is refreshing for me, but I know that I am not going to please everybody. Indeed, I set out to be a little provocative at times and make no apology for so doing.

Stormy Skies starts with a look at past crises so that we can understand the repetitive cyclic behaviour of the industry, the dramatic effect of failure and the desperate need to improve our forecasting abilities. Economic downturns are rather like wars; there is a tendency to believe that there will never be another one. Then, a series of essays covers issues for which airline management needs either a position or a strategy. These are: the risks of overcapacity in the face of unbridled enthusiasm from the original equipment manufacturers; the need to adapt to a world where passenger expectations have radically changed; the dangers, or otherwise, of massive industry consolidation; the perils of airline pricing; the potential of social media; and, naturally, the impact of environmental responsibility on the industry. Finally, some key industry figures gaze into my crystal ball and suggest some challenges we might face ten years hence.

One of my inspirations to address these subjects came from the late Sir Adam Thomson, founder of British Caledonian Airways, who said, 'A recession is when you have to tighten your belt. Depression is when you have no belt to tighten. When you've lost your trousers, you're in the airline business.'

Paul Clark

Chapter 1

'I Should Have Known Better': A History of Crisis and Prediction

Hindsight is a wonderful thing. Yet it is an immutable fact that business leaders, analysts, politicians, soothsayers and gurus throughout the developed world failed to anticipate the impact of the latest economic crisis. More and more countries slipped into recession at the end of 2008 and it seemed as though we were all taken by surprise. It is human nature to conveniently overlook our failings to see the obvious. However, if we take a good look at history we should be prepared to admit that this crisis, like many before, was as inevitable as night follows day. This chapter sets out to appraise the specific events that have regularly dragged the airline business into crisis. We shall see that although previous crises have been very different in nature, a definite pattern of rise and collapse is apparent.

The airline industry is particularly vulnerable to the swings and roundabouts of the global economic system. It walks a permanent tightrope of wafer-thin margins, costs that are increasingly beyond management's realistic control and a demand for its services that is hard to predict. If this were not enough, the cocktail of risk is peppered by the highly competitive nature of the airline business, which drives prices down and leads individual players into endless forays of product investment to keep a grip on market share. Even if we lay aside the spectre of the recession, the airline business is constantly vulnerable to a plethora of potential mini-shocks to the system. Political upheavals, terrorist activity, wars or outbreaks of disease can snap at the heels of airline profits at any time.

We owe it to a nineteenth-century Frenchman, Clément Juglar, who was among the first, if not the first, to correctly identify what we now know as the 'business cycle'. Juglar was a physician as well as an economist and, having lived through the economically-motivated public disturbances of 1848, became interested in how the state of trade influenced the behaviour of the population. By using time-series data he was able to predict the turning points in economic activity (*Encyclopaedia Britannica* 2009). Juglar was the first to observe, for example, that the state of people's bank balances was an indicator of the magnitude of commerce. Sounds familiar? Although Juglar is largely forgotten today, he is revered by economic theorists as being the first to have recorded that the ebb and flow of business activity is indeed a regular phenomenon, and one based on a cycle of roughly 8–11 years. His ground-breaking book, *A Brief History of Panics and Their Periodical Occurrence in the United States*, was first published in 1893 and is still in print today (Juglar 2005). We shall see that the airline industry appears to have fallen neatly in step with the so-called Juglar cycle.

Among the many economists who developed business-cycle theories after Juglar, another stands out. An early twentieth-century Russian economist called Nikolai Kondratiev hit upon the idea that capitalist economies are subject to so-called supercycles that last for an average of 50 years. His theory was actually one of a number that attempt to explain long-term macro-patterns. Such elongated cycles tend to be driven by a variety of major factors such as wars, exceptional crises in the capitalist system or ground-breaking innovations. Kondratiev's ideas were taken up by the leading and prolific Austrian economist Joseph Schumpeter, who devoted seven years of his life at Harvard to produce a 1,000-page monster analysis called, simply, *Business Cycles*, in 1939.

Schumpeter was, by all accounts, a colourful character. He reputedly fought a duel with a librarian over access rights to books for his students and would arrive at faculty meetings dressed in jodphurs and various horseriding paraphenalia. Schumpeter claimed that his ambitions were to be the world's greatest economist, greatest horseman and greatest lover (Perelman 2008). However, of these three ambitions, it was the effort to produce his opus on business cycles that mostly drove him to exhaustion. He wrote to a friend, '"I worried last night till two am on such questions as whether potatoes were important enough in Germany in 1790 to count in the business cycle"' (McCraw 2007). One can easily imagine the exhausted Schumpeter labouring and fretting over his monster tome. Certainly, to his chagrin, the book was never to become a commercial success, but it came to be regarded as a watershed in the history of academic research into economics.

It was Schumpeter who named the elongated cycles 'Kondratiev waves', after the man who identified them. The waves have since re-emerged as the grandly-named Schumpeter–Freeman–Perez paradigm (Freeman and Perez 1988). Essentially, five key waves of high prosperity stand out over the last 200 years (see Figure 1.1). These are: the peak of the Industrial Revolution, the railway boom of the mid-nineteenth century; the emergence of electrical power and predominance of heavy engineering; the impact of motor vehicles, together with the oil economy and mass production; and, finally, the information technology revolution. You may notice a startling omission from this list. The air transport revolution, which so radically altered everyone's lives in the last century, is apparently not deemed significant enough

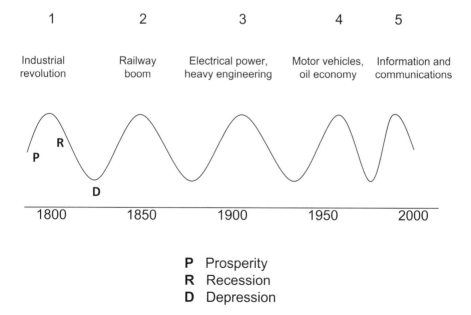

Figure 1.1   Kondratiev waves

to be included. Nevertheless, this theory suggests that we are currently experiencing the cusp of the fifth Kondratiev wave and that a general decline is therefore in prospect. The purity of the Kondratiev waves overlooks the obvious fact that major economic activity is frequently intertwined with major wars, which ignite a potent mixture of opportunity and destruction.

Nikolai Kondratiev's opinions were not shared by his Soviet masters. Stalin believed that Kondratiev waves were critical of his economic strategy and, consequently, the unfortunate economist was sent to a gulag where he came to a sticky end, shot by firing squad in 1938.

There is no shortage of theories that attempt to unravel the mysteries of the business cycle. Analysts have even resorted to the occult and astrology to provide plausible explanations. Thankfully, leading academics have been quick to dismiss quirky fads. One of Schumpeter's students, Professor Paul Samuelson of the Massachusetts Institute of Technology, wrote in his book, *Economics*:

> The business cycle is a pulse common to almost all sectors of economic life and to all capitalistic countries. Movements in national income, unemployment, production prices and profits are not so regular and predictable as the orbits of the planets or the oscillations of a pendulum, and there is no magical method of forecasting the turns of business activity. (Samuelson 1948, p. 408)

No need to explore sunspot theory, then.

Indeed, Samuelson went so far as to blame the emergence of dictatorships and the subsequent Second World War on a failure to address the economic issues that plagued nations during the interwar years. On the other hand, the effects of business cycles have ruined nations, overturned governments, and brought untold suffering to millions and fabulous wealth to a small minority.

The fortunes of the airline industry are obviously closely linked to general business cycles. However, within our industry the various sectors experience a variety of consequences whenever there is a downturn in the economy, and not always in synchronisation. So it should never be presumed that the entire airline industry will suffer in a crisis. Equally, geographical variations can paint a remarkably different picture, depending on where we look. All these phenomena have been observed in previous business cycles. Let's now turn the clock back and see what lessons, if any, can be drawn from the last three global cycles. We shall then examine some violent economic shocks that have affected regions or individual countries and their airlines.

Global Economic Meltdown – The 'Winter of Discontent'

In January 1979 the British Prime Minister, James Callaghan, flew to a four-nation summit held in the French West Indies island of Guadeloupe. In the months prior to his departure the United Kingdom had been in the grip of rising discontent and industrial unrest. When he returned to London Heathrow he was confronted by a bevy of reporters who questioned his judgement in leaving the country in a state of impending chaos. Looking dapper and tanned in a summer suit, James Callaghan brushed off the suggestion that he might consider declaring a state of emergency (BBC 1979). *The Sun* newspaper's headline the next day mocked, 'Crisis, What Crisis?' (*The Sun* 1979). Within no time at all, strikes were causing widespread disruption, heralding the onset of the 'Winter of Discontent'. At the end of March 1979 Mr Callaghan lost a vote of no confidence in the House of Commons and was obliged to call a general election, which he lost to Margaret Thatcher's Conservative Party. History took an alternative turn as a result. 'Crisis, What Crisis?' turned out to be James Callaghan's epitaph, becoming a part of British political folklore, even inspiring an album title by the rock band Supertramp. If any lesson can be drawn from this tale, it is that those who hold responsibility can be guilty of breathtaking folly in the face of blinding truth. But hindsight, as I have already said, is a wonderful thing.

Britain was not the only country experiencing upheaval in 1979. This was the year of the Iranian Revolution, which severely disrupted the global oil market. When Iraq invaded Iran the following year, oil supplies from the region all but ceased. The price of oil was forced up, unleashing widespread panic. All this was coupled with high inflation, high interest rates and a general slowdown in growth in the industrialised nations. Businesses everywhere suffered, and the airline industry was no exception. Of course, 30 years ago airlines were subject to very different regulatory forces than today. One of the high-profile victims of that crisis was Laker Airways, the very first proponent of low-fare travel. Although state ownership was a protective shield for many larger carriers of the day, airlines were nevertheless plunged into their very first major profits crisis.

The crisis of 1979–1981 was the first time that the airline industry, as a whole, made a net operating loss. It was also the first time that a serious imbalance between the supply of capacity into the industry and the appetite to absorb that capacity became apparent. Figure 1.2 shows the relationship between three key industry metrics.

In this figure we can see the numbers of aircraft (of 100 seats or more capacity) being ordered by the world's airlines in the period just prior to the onset of the crisis. The 1970s were characterised by reasonable profits, and, not surprisingly, carriers were anxious to capitalise on their opportunities. As we can see, aircraft orders peaked in 1979. However, profits vanished very quickly beyond this point, and many aircraft ordered in the good times were delivered at the very moment when the airlines were struggling economically. Ironically, demand for air travel was

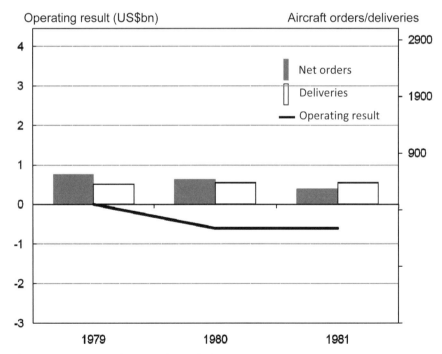

Figure 1.2   Industry in crisis: 1979–1981

Source: Author's data.

hardly affected, although the effect was somewhat masked as the United States was experiencing the first flush of the effects of deregulation at that time.

Undoubtedly, the oil price rises hit the airlines hard, and it was not until fuel prices returned to pre-crisis levels in the mid-1980s that airline profits returned. A close correlation was beginning to emerge between industry profit and aircraft ordering behaviour. This is mostly explained by the rush to keep up with growing demand, but other factors also came into play. First, aircraft orders are driven by replacement cycles, which are themselves determined by economic life-cycle of aircraft. Second, the emergence of new technologies can result in a spate of ordering activity as airlines are keen to grab the keenly contested delivery slots for new aircraft types.

The straightforward message is that even though the demand for air travel was continuing unabated during this major crisis, the airline industry swung violently and unexpectedly from a boom to a bust and then back into a boom period once again.

Global Economic Meltdown – Flight of the Black Swan

Precisely ten years after the previous peak, the next cycle had run its course. But, of course, nobody saw it at the time. And that was understandable as the imminent recession turned out to be an amalgam of a series of events around the globe that individually may not have amounted to much, but together amounted to a great deal.

The first forebodings were in 1987 when an unprecedented collapse of the Dow Jones Industrial Average took place on what was to become known as 'Black Monday'. On a single day in October of that year the Index lost over 22 per cent of its value, seemingly without any warning (Woopidoo 2007). The fact that the ensuing problems in the airline industry can be traced to Black Monday suggests that the cause of the Dow Jones collapse warrants attention. To this day, economists argue over the true cause. A popular explanation is that the crash was a result of so-called 'program trading', which is defined by the New York Stock Exchange as 'a wide range of portfolio trading strategies involving the purchase or sale of fifteen or more stocks having a total market value of US$1 million or more'

(Barron's 2009). It is generally assumed that such trading can only be handled by computers, and that the rapid acceleration of stock-selling on that fateful day was exacerbated by an automated process that simply ran out of control.

However, recent analysis of Black Monday suggests a more sinister explanation and one that, if plausible, could present huge challenges for those attempting to predict the future. A former Wall Street options trader called Nassim Nicholas Taleb has suggested that Black Monday was an event categorised as a 'Black Swan' (Taleb 2007). The idea is that there is a presumption that all swans are white, so that a black swan is a metaphor for something that did not exist and could not have existed before its actual appearance. In other words, when there is a sighting of a black swan it comes as a complete surprise, but we convince ourselves that we knew about its existence all along. Taleb postulates that a Black Swan event is something that has high impact and is totally unpredictable and undirected. An example of such an event would be the 11 September 2001 attacks. He argues that a person advocating the design of reinforced cockpit doors would have had a hard time before 9/11. Yet the absence of reinforced doors was a key reason why the attacks could be perpetrated.

Hindsight compels us to try to predict the known unknowns. In other words, we are accustomed to taking account of highly improbable, but possible, eventualities. But if we are to believe in Black Swans we are compelled to accept that, no matter how sophisticated the modelling technique, we will never be able to correctly anticipate the totally unpredictable or, as Donald Rumsfeld once ineloquently put it, the unknown unknowns (Rumsfeld 2002).

In the days following Black Monday in 1987, and to everyone's relief, the stock market rallied and it seemed as though the crisis had been averted. But the simmering spectre of the the failure of the US savings and loans associations fuelled a growing alarm. The United States quickly ran into budget problems as it struggled, along with taxpayers, to bail out the savings and loans businesses. Then, there was a squeeze in the real-estate market. At lightning speed the North American economy slipped into recession, dragging along those countries most closely linked to the United States. For a while it seemed as though catastrophe had been averted as consumer spending remained unexpectedly high.

But the Iraqi invasion of Kuwait towards the end of 1990 put paid to any hopes of a quick recovery. The price of oil briefly soared, taking inflation with it, and the ensuing problems of budget deficit and high unemployment returned with a vengeance.

In other parts of the world, recession occurred for very different reasons. For example, Finland was plunged into deep recession in 1991 as a result of the loss of most of its trade with its neighbour, Russia, in the wake of the collapse of the Soviet Union. Both Australia and New Zealand experienced recession at the same time, but other factors, such as the pace of reform and alleged government mismanagement of the economy, were largely to blame.

The airline industry bore the brunt of the problem. Major companies such as Eastern Airlines and Pan American Airways disappeared. In Europe we saw the collapse of Air Europe. Of the world's top 20 airlines, only British Airways, Swissair, Cathay Pacific and Singapore Airlines were consistently profitable from 1991 to 1993 (Doganis 2002). Many airlines survived only due to capital injections or, in the case of some European carriers, state aid.

Figure 1.3 reveals a starkly similar pattern to the problems of the previous recession.

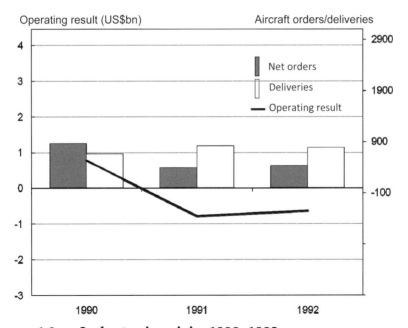

Figure 1.3   Industry in crisis: 1990–1992

Source: Author's data.

Here we see an erosion of profitability following a period of record orders for aircraft capacity, and we see much of that capacity being delivered at a time the airlines least need it. However, two new features emerged. For the first time in the history of civil aviation there was a year-on-year drop in the numbers of passengers carried, from 1990 to 1991. Second, a large percentage of the aircraft capacity ordered prior to the collapse in profits was ordered by the newly-emerging leasing companies, which had been quick to grab delivery slots from willing manufacturers in order to make a killing through short-term operating leases. The failure and reconstitution of Guinness Peat Aviation as GECAS, or General Electric Commercial Aviation Services, was probably the most memorable shake-out of those troubled times. This was the time when the Mojave desert began to fill up with scores of unwanted aircraft, most of them already old and economically inefficent, but some brand-new. If ever we needed a testimony to overoptimism in the airline industry, the Mojave desert provided one.

The lesson from the 1990–1992 recession was crystal-clear. History does, indeed, repeat itself. But, if the event that triggered the recession was indeed a Black Swan, then this could undermine classical business cycle theory. Somehow, it seems, we need to hone our skills in predicting the unpredictable.

Global Economic Meltdown – The Recession We Almost Never Had

I remember sitting in a meeting in the Airbus headquarters in the summer of 2001, when the subject of discussion was the unexpectedly poor performance of the air cargo sector in the second quarter of that year. Was this the precursor to a recession, we all asked ourselves? Indeed, it was quite logical to presume that the health of the air cargo business would act as a barometer for the entire industry. And so it proved. However, throughout the autumn of that year pundits were arguing that there might not, in fact, be a recession at all. There was much talk of a 'soft landing'. But the airlines were already suffering. A strong dollar and high fuel prices were already enough to trigger profit warnings. However, the collapse, when it came, was from completely unexpected quarters.

Unquestionably, the Black Swan of 11 September 2001 precipitated a global crisis of unprecedented intensity. Yet, somewhat surprisingly, the 2001 recession was remarkably short-lived as far as the United States was concerned. At least, this is according to the official arbiter of business cycle dating, the National Bureau of Economic Research, which decided that the recession was already over by November 2001 (NBER 2001). However, by this time Ansett Australia, Swissair, Sabena and Canada 3000 had already collapsed, and losses were beginning to pile up for the world's airlines.

Figure 1.4 reveals the relationship between airline profitability, aircraft ordering behaviour and aircraft deliveries around the 2001 crisis. In fact, profits were beginning to tumble as early as 1999. But this hardly put a dent in the order books in Seattle and Toulouse. When the crisis came, once again airlines were faced with capacity they did not need or want.

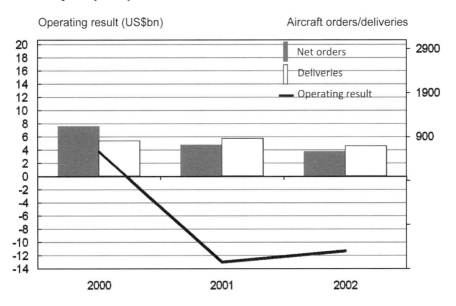

Figure 1.4   Industry in crisis: 200–2002

Source: Author's data.

One of the popular phrases being bandied about Airbus at the time was 'deep-V recovery'. The idea was that the misfortunes of the airline industry were the result of a cataclysmic and unforseeable event and the good times would return almost as quickly as they had disappeared. In itself, this seemed a plausible enough proposition. Indeed, the forecasters dreamt up the idea of visualising the collapse of passenger traffic in 2001 as following exactly the same pattern as the collapse of 1991. It followed, they would argue, that recovery must follow the same course. However, recovery of air travel demand to pre-crisis levels was about to be hit by a sequence of regional events that stoked up more agony for the poor airlines.

The last three major global crises have been driven mostly by events that have taken place in the developed world, especially in the United States and Europe. Now we must turn our attention to other nations and assess how their economic woes have spilled over into the airline industry. These other nations have had, and will continue to have, an impact on us all.

Whither the Tiger Economies?

It must be irksome to nations in the developing world that news, opinion and attitude all seem to emanate from the United States. This is partly understandable in that the United States exerts considerable influence, especially in business and finance, and data is quite readily available. It is also true to say that American civil aviation is dominant. However, in the course of the twenty-first century this is likely to change, and the influence of other nations will become more predominant. This will be especially true of the resurgent and surging economies of Russia, India and China, for example.

In terms of the airline industry, these emerging nations tend to figure rather less in conventional thinking simply because the amount of traffic they currently generate is relatively minor in comparison to the might of the United States or Europe. For example, the continent of Africa offers up no more than 3 per cent of global air traffic and for South America the figure is 5 per cent (Airbus 2007). In terms of gross domestic product (GDP), the figures are 3.7 per cent and 7.7 per cent respectively (CIA 2008). There have been numerous regional crises that have had a dramatic effect on those airlines affected, as well as carriers domiciled in the larger markets.

Between the 1990–1992 and 2001–2002 global crises a major financial crisis gripped practically all of the Asian economies. Many countries in the region had been enjoying considerable expansion and GDP annual growth rates of a torrid 10 per cent or more throughout most of the 1990s. Some economists, notably Nobel Prize winner Paul Krugman, had identified as early as 1994 that true long-term prosperity would not be assured until total factor productivity equalled the high amounts of capital flowing into the Asian economies (Krugman 1994). Krugman postulated that the success of nations such as Singapore was based largely on the mobilisation of resources rather than other factors such as technology development and improvements in efficiency. His article sounded a strident cautionary note that the Asian economic miracle was not all that it was cracked up to be. Indeed, so it proved.

The first signs of trouble occurred in Thailand, where overborrowing had weakened the economy to the point where the country was approaching bankruptcy. Quite suddenly, in May 1997, the Thai baht was battered by speculative attacks. Within weeks the baht, which had been pegged to the US dollar, was floated, and went on to lose one-third of its value. These events sparked off a general financial meltdown throughout the region, with South Korea and Indonesia faring particularly badly. The ensuing loss of confidence was felt in Hong Kong, the Philippines, Singapore, Malaysia, Vietnam, Japan and the People's Republic of China. The US dollar value of the GNP of Thailand, Indonesia, Philippines, Malaysia and South Korea fell by an astonishing 46 per cent in the period from June 1997 to July 1998 (Cheetham 1998). The International Monetary Fund stepped in with packages to aid and prop up many of the ailing economies.

Given the clear link between GDP growth and air travel demand, the airlines, unsurprisingly, all suffered to one degree or another. Business travel was severely curtailed within the region for a while. Those carriers highly dependent on intra-Asian traffic suffered because their revenues were denominated in the collapsing local currencies. But their expenses, comprising operating costs and debt, were denominated in increasingly expensive dollars. Airlines in Indonesia and Korea very quickly fell victim to this effect, whereas airlines with global networks, such as Singapore Airlines, were able to rely on revenues paid in currencies other than those of the weakened Asian nations, and so fared rather better. Survival was only possible due to government intervention and the redeployment of capacity to more lucrative long-haul markets, where traffic rights permitted. Even well-managed and highly successful airlines could not escape the problems. Cathay Pacific Airways experienced its first loss in 35 years, for example, and saw its yield erode by almost 19 per cent in 1998 (Cathay Pacific 1999). The airline nevertheless held its nerve and absorbed ten new wide-bodied aircraft into the fleet and opened new routes to Istanbul and San Francisco, where market opportunities were not affected by the turmoil in Asia.

Despite Asia's woes, on a global scale the crisis was seen as little more than a severe bout of flu, rather than a case for hospitalisation. Indeed, the crisis is referred to as 'Asian Flu'. The global upward progression of traffic hardly missed a step. Nevertheless, the crisis proved once again that the airline industry was not immune to a sudden external shock to the system. What was more worrying was that the crisis was by no means a Black Swan. Krugman had seen it coming almost four years earlier. It seemed as though the 'newly industrialising countries' were paper tigers after all.

Two Financial Hotspots

It was not only Asia that experienced a bout of illness at the end of the 1990s. Russia managed to create constant alarm by failing to live up to post-Soviet expectations. Its weak economy was highly dependent on the price of oil which declined to such a point towards the end of the decade as to put severe pressure on the economy. But it was, unsurprisingly, a financial crisis which finally caused the economy to snap. In 1998 the ruble virtually collapsed, along with the banking sector, and for a while it seemed as though the promise of a new Russia would never be achieved. However, a rise in energy prices in 1999 helped Russia recover relatively quickly. Aeroflot Russian International Airlines was not immune to the difficulties and suffered a reported loss of US$211 million in 1998, having made a profit of US$305 million the previous year (*St Petersburg Times* 2009).

Confidence in Latin American economies was badly shaken by successive financial crises in Mexico, Brazil and Argentina. A familiar pattern took hold in Argentina, where years of rising international debt, rising unemployment and falling GDP signalled a recession in 1999. On the advice of the International Monetary Fund, and in an effort to combat hyperinflation, Argentina adopted a fixed exchange rate policy by which the peso was pegged at the same rate as the US dollar. However, this simply provoked another problem as the peso increased in value along with the dollar during the boom years of the mid-1990s. Argentina's major trading partners were Brazil and Europe, but the Brazilian real and the euro were valued at a lower rate than the peso. This had the effect of halting Argentina's export market and therefore the growth of the economy. As panic took hold, people started withdrawing large sums from the banks, leading to all bank accounts being effectively frozen for a period of 12 months. Just when it seemed that things could not get any worse, a public uprising forced the government to impose a state of emergency, which itself provoked serious rioting, leaving several people dead. By 2002 employment was hovering at around 25 per cent, and it looked as though Argentina was heading for complete collapse. It was only through a complete change in government policy and a radical change in the outlook for Argentina's exports, especially soy, that the country stabilised once more.

Needless to say, the country's airlines suffered. The national carrier, Aerolíneas Argentinas, was already in a parlous state before the country's financial crisis took hold. In 2001 the company went into administration and fell under the control of a Spanish consortium. Eventually, the airline's debt was restructured and the company was renationalised in 2008.

The China Enigma

In 1991 I made several visits to China and spent time speaking to airlines about the economic problems that were enveloping the world's airline industry at the time. On the one hand, it was gratifying that the Chinese airlines were keen to form a better understanding of the economic forces at work elsewhere in the world. On the other hand, I quickly realised that my Chinese hosts considered themselves to be totally immune from the kind of problems befalling other airlines at the time. Indeed, they were quite affronted at the suggestion that there was such a thing as a global airline industry. I was told, very politely, that the five-year plan would be adhered to, no matter what. Essentially, 'it is written'.

It was a very different story two years earlier when I found myself as the sole business-class passenger on a British Airways 747 from Hong Kong to Beijing just three days after the Tiananmen Square protests. The uncertainty following that particular Black Swan had quelled practically all travel by foreigners to China but, to my surprise, domestic flights were packed as usual.

Yet in 2001, on another tour of Chinese airlines, I was once again told that the woes of the world's airlines would not affect China's determination to adhere to the current five-year plan. However, China can no longer assert total immunity from the economic problems facing the rest of the world.

The Spectre of SARS

The death of a farmer, in Guangdong Province, China, towards the end of November 2002 heralded the arrival of another Black Swan. This one took the form of a virulent respiratory disease called SARS, or Severe Acute Respiratory Syndrome. By the time the epidemic calmed towards the middle of 2003, a total of 774 deaths had been officially reported by the World Health Organisation (WHO 2004). Apart from numerous Asian countries, Canada and the United States were particularly affected.

The effect on air travel was astonishing. The flight scheduling provider, the OAG (Official Airline Guide), announced that the virus had had a greater effect on the global airline industry than the war with Iraq. It reported a 45 per cent decline in numbers of flights scheduled to and from China in the period June 2002 to June 2003. Hong Kong's airport authority reported an 80 per cent drop in traffic at Hong Kong airport compared to the previous year. What was more surprising was the scale of the crisis in worldwide terms. The number of scheduled flights fell by 3 per cent over this period, representing a loss of 2.5 million seats.

With tourism slowing to a trickle, Cathay Pacific Airways had no choice but to ground aircraft, cutting 45 per cent of its flying programme (BBC 2003a). Qantas reported that all aspects of its operations had been affected and implemented cost-cutting measures and staff lay-offs. Airlines in Europe fared little better. KLM announced that Asia-Pacific traffic flows dropped by 24 per cent (BBC 2003b).

Coming hard on the heels of the effects of the wars in Iraq and Afghanistan, the airline industry was rightly asking the question 'Whatever next?' The 'deep-V' recovery after the attacks of 11 September 2001 turned out to be nothing more than a myth.

The Grandaddy of Them All

Pundits tell us, rather too gleefully, that the most recent airline crisis is the worst that the industry has ever faced, precipitated by a global economic crisis of gargantuan proportions. It is always easy to be wise after the event, but it is astonishing that financial experts failed to heed the warning signals of an oncoming economic meltdown. Major financial institutions such as Freddie Mac, Fannie Mae and AIG had suffered billion-dollar losses before the tipping point of the collapse of Lehman was reached. Until this point, the financial community failed to realise that it was riding on a runaway train, blanking previous crises from memory. How could no-one have noticed that a mountain of debt, coupled with a greed culture of short-term rewards, was bound to end in disaster? Although it is easy to heap blame on the financiers, one can argue that corporate chiefs, rating agencies, regulators, shareholders, investors and even borrowers were all swept along on a wave of collective blindness and disbelief. Either the global economic crisis of 2007–2009 was another Black Swan, or a severe case of financial institution dementia. Daniel Sallier, a professional air transport forecaster, argues, 'The system will keep working as long as creditors believe in economic strength. If creditors lose confidence then the system will collapse.'

Figure 1.5 reveals that the long-suffering airline industry has been repeating the same old pattern of reluctantly absorbing

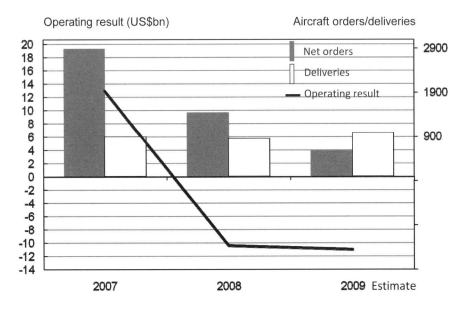

Figure 1.5   Industry in crisis: 2007–2009

new aircraft capacity that had been ordered in good times. Critics will jump up and argue that many new deliveries were supporting developing economies, as well as low-cost carriers which remained largely profitable when others were failing. Also, goes the argument, new aircraft – even with financing costs considered – deliver better operating economics than the aircraft they replace. I completely agree. But we cannot escape the fact that there is considerable inertia inherent in an air transportation system where capacity can never be brought in or, far more critically, be taken out quickly enough in response to rapidly evolving demand. This is especially true for aircraft capacity, but also applies to airport and even airspace capacity. The ability of the providers and users of capacity to work together to provide solutions in the interests of every player in the business becomes crucial. Whether behaviour of this nature is termed collusion or cooperation is a moot point. The fact of the matter is that capacity management of the air transport system is not coordinated.

It is not the purpose of this book to pick through the rubble of so many collapsed airlines. Frankly, it would be too depressing and would not serve our purpose. Instead, we should step back and survey the whole sorry battlefield and ask ourselves whether the strategic approach of the entire airline industry has been faulty. It certainly seems as though the airline industry is destined to fall flat on its face every time the global economy crumbles. But why should it always be like this? Should we have known better? My answer to this question is a definite 'yes'.

In Conclusion

Different factors triggered each of economic downturns that have periodically wrecked so many airlines. However, there is a pattern at work, as the global economy is apt to oscillate between periods of prosperity and periods of difficulty in cycles of approximately ten years. These waves appear to follow Clément Juglar's ideas of the periodic business cycle. In addition to the global cycles, there have been a series of regional ripples within the general wave that have had dramatic local effects. These 'satellite crises' have spilled over to affect the global picture, but only to a limited degree. Recovery from such satellite crises has always been rapid.

The airline business can be characterised as a balancing act between fickle and volatile demand on one hand, and a production process that carries high cost, much of it beyond direct control of management, on the other. Owing to relatively thin margins the industry is particularly susceptible to the fall-out from worsening economic or financial conditions. Yet, despite obvious advance warning signals of impending problems, the industry has consistently failed to prepare itself for the onslaught of a worsening economic environment. These failures appear to come from a combination of optimism and an unwillingness to accept that times will ever turn bad again. The philosopher Georg Hegel wrote:

> What experience and history teach us is that people and governments have never learned anything from history, nor acted upon any lessons they might have drawn from it. (Hegel 1988[1837], p. 8)

We need only substitute 'airlines' for 'people and governments' and the quotation rings true for the airline industry. Even more telling are the words of the philosopher George Santanyana, who wrote in *The Life of Reason*:

Those who cannot remember the past are condemned to repeat it. (Santayana 1905)

To be fair, even the most robust forecasting processes would not have been able to foresee the Black Swans that have wreaked havoc with the smooth continuum so favoured by the forecasters. Yet unpredictable events may unleash consequences equal in magnitude to those of the natural business cycles.

How can we fly past these stormy skies with minimal turbulence? If our world is about to enter another Kondratiev wave in the course of this century, the airline industry needs to be better prepared, for both long-term and short-term shocks and bumps. The rest of this book will address some of the key emerging business challenges that airlines will need to confront. Acknowledging and adapting to these challenges could make the different between survival and failure when turbulence threatens. The first of these is something of an old chestnut: the perpetual optimism of the aircraft manufacturers and their drive to feed the world's airlines with capacity, and the ease with which airlines happily absorb this capacity, only to find themselves suffering regular bouts of severe indigestion.

References

Airbus, 2007. *Flying by Nature: Global Market Forecast 2007–2026.* Available at: http://stagev4.airbus.com/store/mm_repository/pdf/att00011423/media_object_file_GMF_2007.pdf. (accessed 19 May 2010).

Barron's, 2009. 'NYSE Program Trading'. 24 May. Available at: http://online.barrons.com/public/page/9_0210-nysepgtd.html (accessed 21 April 2009).

BBC, 1979. '"No Chaos Here" Declares Callaghan'. Available (including video) at: http://news.bbc.co.uk/onthisday/hi/dates/stories/january/ 10/newsid_2518000/2518957.stm (accessed 21 April 2009).

BBC, 2003a. 'Sars Hit Airlines "More Than War"'. 13 June. Available at: http://news.bbc.co.uk/2/hi/business/2986612.stm (accessed 22 April 2009).

BBC, 2003b. 'Sars Hits KLM's Asian Routes. 5 May. Available at: http://news.bbc.co.uk/2/hi/business/3000951.stm (accessed 22 April 2009).

Cathay Pacific, 1999. Press release, 10 March 1999. Available at: http://www.irasia.com/listco/hk/cathay/annual/98/respress.htm (accessed 22 April 2009).

Cheetham, R., 1998. 'Asia Crisis'. Paper presented at US-ASEAN-Japan Policy Dialogue conference. School of Advanced International Studies of Johns Hopkins University, Washington, DC, 7–9 June 1998.

CIA, 2008. *World Factbook*. Washington, DC: US Central Intelligence Agency.

Doganis, R., 2002. *Flying Off Course: The Economics of International Airlines*. Third edition. London: Routledge.

Encyclopædia Britannica, 2009. 'Clément Juglar'. Available at: http://www. britannica.com/EBchecked/topic/307658/Clement-Juglar (accessed 15 April 2009).

Freeman, C. and Perez, C., 1988. 'Structural Crises of Adjustment, Business Cycles and Investment Behaviour'. In G. Dosi, R. Nelson, Silverberg, G. and L. Soete (eds), *Technical Change and Economic Theory*. London and New York: Pinter Publishers, 38–66.

Hegel, G., 1988[1837]. *Introduction to the Philosophy of History*. Trans Leo Rauch. Indianapolis, ID: Hackett.

Juglar, C., 2005. *A Brief History of Panics in the United States*, New York: Cosimo Classics.

Krugman, P., 1994. 'The Myth of Asia's Miracle'. *Foreign Affairs*, 73(6), 62–78.

McCraw, T.K., 2007. *Prophet of Innovation: Joseph Schumpeter and Creative Destruction*. Cambridge, MA: Harvard University Press.

NBER, 2001. 'Business Cycle Expansions and Contractions'. Available at: http://www.nber.org/cycles.html (accessed 21 April 2009).

Perelman, M., 2008. 'Two Degrees of Separation: Reflections on Stolper and Schumpeter'. 17 May. Available at: http://michaelperelman.wordpress. com/2008/05/17/two-degrees-of-separation-reflections-on-stolper-and-schumpeter (accessed 21 April 2009).

Rumsfeld, D., 2002. 'Press Conference by US Secretary of State, Donald Rumsfeld'. NATO, Brussels, 7 June. Available at: http://www.nato.int/ docu/speech/2002/s020606g.htm (accessed 21 April 2009).

Samuelson, P., 1948. *Economics*. New York: McGraw-Hill/Irwin.

Schumpeter, J.A., 1939. *Business Cycles: A Theoretical, Historical and Statistical Analysis of the Capitalist Process*. New York and London: McGraw-Hill.

The Sun, 1979. Editorial. 11 January.

St Petersburg Times, 2009. 'Long-Serving Aeroflot CEO Replaced with Sistema Executive'. 31 March. Available at: http://www.sptimes.ru/index. php?action_id=2&story_id=28643 (accessed 22 April 2009).

Taleb, N., 2007. *The Black Swan: The Impact of the Highly Improbable*. New York: Random House.

WHO, 2004. 'Summary of Probable SARS Cases with Onset of Illness from 1 November 2002 to 31 July 2003'. Available at: http://www.who.int/csr/ sars/country/table2004_04_21/en/index.html (accessed 22 April 2009).

Woopidoo Business Glossary, 1987. 'Black Monday 1987'. Available at: http:// www.woopidoo.com/glossary/black-monday/index.htm (accessed 27 December 2009).

Chapter 2

'Tomorrow Never Knows': Forecasting Aircraft Capacity

Christmas 1985. The staff canteen at Airbus headquarters in Toulouse. The company's colourful president, Jean Pierson, stood on a small improvised platform before the entire complement of Airbus staff, numbering around 1,000. The engineers, contract negotiators, marketing analysts and support staff craned their necks for a view of the affable Pierson, as he prepared to give his seasonal address to the troops. Pierson was renowned for a gruff manner mixed with Gallic petulance, and a tendency to mispronounce English words, sometimes with comical effect. The expectant crowd was duly rewarded with a vintage Pierson performance, as he delivered a characteristically flamboyant attack on the mighty Boeing which then commanded a massive and seemingly unassailable share of the aircraft market. Then Pierson did something unexpected. He paused for effect and looked directly at his audience. Gripping the side of the rostrum, he leaned forward and said, slowly and deliberately, and with a heavy accent, 'Ladies and gentlemen, mark my words. One day we shall be Number One.' But there was no cheering, no whooping or even nodding of heads. Instead there were some murmurs and whispered exchanges, but mostly private disbelief that this upstart of a company could ever aspire to overthrow the mighty Americans.

The rest, as they say, is history.

The Art of the Crystal Ball

Airbus and Boeing have always held consistently close views on the growth of air transport demand. This is not especially surprising, as air travel demand is largely driven by forecasts of general parameters such as the economy, disposable income, the price of oil and so on. As long as the independent variables are broadly similar we should not expect manufacturer forecasts to differ significantly. The success of individual manufacturers is a function of their ability to satisfy forecast demand for aircraft through their product lines, the technologies they deploy, the operating performance, economics and availabilities of these products, their respective opinions of how passengers make travel choices and how airlines perceive their capacity needs. The only area where there has been a difference of opinion concerns the market for aircraft larger than 400 seats. And it is a fundamental difference. Essentially, Airbus is a believer in the notion that traffic will be channelled through major hubs, leading to the need for around 1,832 large passenger and cargo aircraft over the next 20 years, while acknowledging the need for smaller aircraft to serve fragmenting markets served by variants of the A350 (Airbus 2009a). Boeing's conviction is that the demand for very large aircraft is much more limited, and it has placed its principle bet on the longer-range 787 family, choosing to develop the 747-8 for the more marginal high-capacity market which it estimates as just 740 units over 20 years. Significantly, this value had been reduced from an estimate of 980 units just one year earlier, as Boeing sees a reduction in the cargo market affecting the number of large-capacity aircraft (Boeing 2009).

Conversely, Airbus actually saw fit to increase its overall long-term view of the market's appetite for capacity. So the *Global Market Forecast 2009–2028* suggested that 689 additional aircraft, or 2.8 per cent of total orders, would be needed over the ensuing 20 years. The rationale for this optimism was the simple point that projected high fuel prices would induce airlines to replace their fleets of less fuel-efficient aircraft more quickly (Airbus 2009a). If you think about it, it's a reasonable idea, although a critic might argue that this is another example of a manufacturer 'talking up' the market.

Both sides dug their heels in with their divergent market opinions as far back as the mid-1990s when the two companies even held talks on jointly producing a large-capacity aircraft before Boeing, becoming convinced that the market did not really want large aircraft, pulled out owing to cost and risk. The consequence of these diverging views led to the evolution of very different product offerings, especially in terms of capacity, and raises probably the biggest chicken-and-egg question ever in the history of aircraft manufacturing.

Big is Beautiful, I Think

There is a classic aphorism, stated by the sociologist William Isaac Thomas, which goes like this: 'If men define situations as real, they become real in their consequences' (Thomas 1928).

Here is some conventional thinking. You take a good look at the market and decide what capacity the airline industry will need, then design and build an aircraft family to support that need. Sounds reasonable? Now look at it this way. You form a genuine conviction about what aircraft types may be required in the future, formulate a product development strategy to support that need, and then orient your view of the market to bolster that product development strategy. Although a simplification, it is tempting to imagine such a game being played out in long-haul markets. It is legitimate to question whether manufacturers' forecasts are, at least to some extent, self-fulfilling prophecies. After all, once you have committed billions of dollars to the development of a particular size of aircraft, it stands to reason that the company risks becoming wedded to the market justification of the decision. I am not singling out any particular manufacturer, but you only have to consult the record of sales brochures, presentations and press conferences to see that trend. I put this point to Randy Tinseth, Boeing's Vice President Marketing. Unsurprisingly, Randy was never going to agree with me. He paused and then responded in quiet, measured tones, 'We think that the forecast, technology and conversations with your customers should drive your strategy; we don't think that your strategy should be driven by your products.'

When it comes to the very high-capacity aircraft market, the simple truth is that neither Boeing nor Airbus can be completely right. Even the perennially optimistic Chief Commercial Officer of Airbus, John Leahy, has been quoted as saying that either the

A380 will become the flagship of the twenty-first century or it will be a disaster. Former Boeing boss Phil Condit once said much the same thing. Industry consultant Richard Aboulafia of the Teal Group was more damning, describing the A380 as a 'big mistake' (Wallace 2007). Boeing's Randy Tinseth points out that it is the market that speaks. He argues that 747-8 sales have tracked A380 sales virtually unit for unit, with Boeing having sold 100 of their product in five years compared to 200 A380 sales in ten years: 'I want to understand from Airbus why the market hasn't evolved the way they said. They've got some explaining to do.' Christian Scherer is Executive Vice President and Head of Strategy and Future Programmes at Airbus. His belief in the need for large aircraft is based on a simple and compelling argument: 'There are two vectors of productivity improvement; one is speed, and that's going nowhere because of the exponential costs of energy associated with increasing speed, as well as a natural wall called the sound barrier. The only other vector of improvement is size.'

Let's admit it – no-one knows the true size of the market for very large aircraft. The only certainty is that the large-capacity aircraft forecast of one of the two giant manufacturers must be plain wrong. Yet there is little point in agonising over the next 20 years when faced with so much difficulty in today's market. Although it is absolutely necessary for suppliers to forecast over the very long term due to the enormous timescales and inertia in aircraft design and development, current woes dictate that the manufacturers shift their focus to management of their order book, assuring current deliveries and helping customers arrange finance. After all, even if product strategies are divergent, everyone is in the same boat today.

Crisis, What Crisis?

Although new aircraft orders understandably slowed in 2009, the manufacturers are sticking doggedly to their long-term average forecast growth numbers, believing that periodic crises are merely blips in a trend of inexorable growth. Those airlines affected by crisis will clearly lose their appetite for deliveries of previously ordered aircraft. The manufacturers are naturally dependent on the global market to absorb the capacity under current production, but must obviously be prepared to be flexible with customers who seek deferrals. At the same time, maintaining a stable rate of production is desirable for the industrial process to run smoothly.

However, some industry specialists were pessimistic at the beginning of 2009 when it came to predicting deliveries. For example IATA, an organisation that assumed the mantle of announcing constant bad news about the airline crisis in 2009, was widely quoted as believing that Boeing and Airbus would deliver less than half of aircraft in production for 2009, on the basis that financing would be too hard to come by (Sobie 2009). IATA's was not the only voice of doom. Leasing companies, such as Dubai Aerospace Enterprises and International Lease Finance Corporation (ILFC), were far from reassured that buyers were financially secure enough to take possession of aircraft. ILFC's former chief executive, Steven Udvar-Hazy, quipped that when a bomb explodes, the light travels faster than the sound, but the flash occurred in September 2008 and the sound had yet to be heard in either Seattle or Toulouse (Gates 2009). Udvar-Hazy also predicted that manufacturers would cut deliveries by as much as 35 per cent from the fourth quarter of 2008 onwards (Rothman and Ray 2009). If you think about it, the world's largest civil aircraft leasing organisation is in the business of aircraft value speculation, and the last thing ILFC would want to see is oversupply of capacity. The ideal scenario is to place a large order, corner the market and hope that production comes to a standstill. Other key companies in the aircraft supply chain also publicly voiced their concern that production rates were too high. The chief executive of Boeing's key 737 aircraft supplier, Spirit Aerospace Systems, was reported as being 'terribly worried' about the reluctance of Boeing and Airbus to cut back production sufficiently owing to the crisis (Ostrower 2009). Again, this view comes as no surprise as Spirit was once effectively a division of Boeing and understands the trauma of wildly fluctuating production rates.

There are two basic reasons why airline customers seek to defer or cancel aircraft orders in a time of crisis. First, they must obviously reduce capacity in line with demand. But, second, customers have to overcome the challenge of finding the finance to pay for the aircraft. The US federal Export-Import Bank announced that it was willing to offer up to US$10 billion in guarantees to help finance US-made aircraft destined for overseas customers (Gates 2009).

As it happened, IATA's dramatic prediction of a massive delivery shortfall in 2009 turned out to be quite wrong, and both Airbus and Boeing almost precisely met their delivery targets. Says Airbus's Scherer, 'We have maintained our outflow of aircraft without having to renegotiate our deals or refinance aircraft in any extraordinary manner.' He quickly adds, 'But we're auditing our backlog like hot milk on a fire.'

Figures 2.1 and 2.2 indicate that net orders were significantly and understandably reduced as the crisis took hold. In 2009 a total of 979 aircraft were delivered by the Boeing and Airbus juggernaut into an airline industry that was globally on its knees.

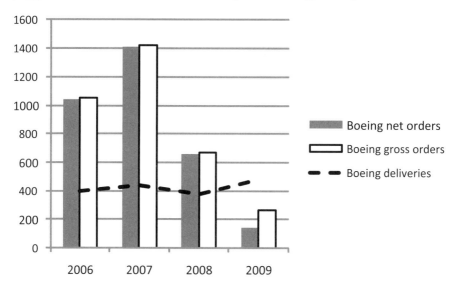

Figure 2.1   Orders and deliveries: Boeing, 2006–2009

Source: Manufacturers' reports.

The manufacturers were undoubtedly relieved by this amazing performance and, as is their custom, they continue to trumpet the astonishing size of their overall backlog, which amounts to 3,375 units for Boeing, and 3,488 units for Airbus. It is difficult to estimate the value of this gigantic combined figure due to the obvious fact that actual pricing is confidential. However, a

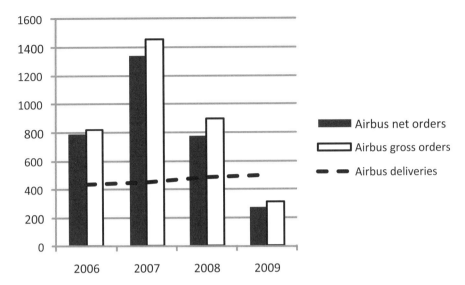

Figure 2.2   Orders and deliveries: Airbus, 2006–2009

Source: Manufacturers' reports.

reasonable estimate is that Boeing and Airbus are looking forward to an income bonanza worth around US$750 billion within the next seven years. And all this to support an airline industry that historically has struggled to generate any positive return on capital invested at all. It is a fallacy, incidentally, that a robust order book can sustain a manufacturer during a downturn. If customers cannot accept current deliveries, then a healthy backlog cannot possibly insulate the manufacturers from the short-term effects of crisis. Yet, on the back of a contract executed in good faith but ultimately hard to enforce if the going gets tough, plus a relatively small down payment and a large dose of goodwill, the manufacturer will launch the production process of an aircraft. It really is a risky business.

Timing is Everything

Designing, developing and building aircraft is a long-winded process, and one that moves at a slower pace than the dynamic world of the airline business. The aircraft and engine builders cannot allow short-term vagaries of the market to interfere with their long-term strategies. This is why their forecasts stretch over decades and focus on trends, rather than on punctual and sharp fluctuations of a market in crisis. The decision to develop a new aircraft type is driven by myriad parameters. Assessments are made of the overall nature of the demand for air travel, macro-economic parameters such as the price of fuel and other essential costs, and industry-specific trends such as the likely evolution of airport infrastructure and regulatory shifts. These analyses will reveal the scope of potential demand for a certain amount of aircraft capacity which may need to be satisfied by various combinations of aircraft sizes and range capability. There is nothing particularly controversial about this 'textbook' list.

However, there are two much more fundamental ingredients to product strategy decisions. The first concerns the degree of innovation that may be successfully and economically woven into a particular product line. The release of new technology is driven by impetus to innovate from the market as well as competing suppliers, the level of acceptable risk, cost of development, expected reliability, market acceptance, the economic benefit to suppliers and customers, and the perceived competitive edge by buyers. The second vital ingredient concerns the *timing* of the introduction of a new aircraft model. This is a much more complex issue and may be determined by the impact of a new technology on the asset value of existing models, the potential appetite of customers to assume their share of the risk and, crucially, an assessment of where the existing models of competing suppliers are positioned within their respective product life-cycles. A positive perception of an aircraft model that is currently selling well can change instantly when, for example, a replacement is announced or, even worse, when a freighter conversion programme is discussed. Such talk is akin to signing your own death warrant.

The Leapfrog Game

The American civil aircraft suppliers had the field to themselves when Jean Pierson was telling his staff in the Airbus canteen that they could become the number one manufacturer. It was only when Airbus had established its reputation as a technology innovator with the A320 family that buyers began to perceive

'Tomorrow Never Knows'   31

the technology leapfrog. The early Airbus wide-bodied aircraft were more than matched by Boeing's 767 – especially in its more developed versions. However, the A320 family was markedly superior to the original 737 design until Boeing caught up with the next-generation (NG) variants. Airbus designed the A320 from a blank sheet of paper, which carried an advantage of being unhampered by legacy, although Boeing enjoyed a head-start in that particular market segment in terms of sales volume and installed customer base. The immediate perception was that Airbus was the technology innovator and Boeing was forced to catch up by introducing incremental improvements to the original 737. Over time the A320 and 737NG families gravitated to a kind of equilibrium in which the products were more closely matched in terms of performance and economics. Similarly, in the wide-bodied market Airbus struck the first blow with its A340 and A330 families, leaving Boeing to catch up with the 777 series which it introduced several years later. Once again, the performance characteristics of the multitude of models in this size and range category converged over time.

Over a period of several decades the two major manufacturers took different paths in technology but nevertheless ended up with aircraft families that competed head-to-head with each other and are frankly not very far away from each other in terms of operating economics and performance. The potential to converge can even be observed with the next generation of twin-aisle aircraft, the 787 and A350. Several large airlines have opted for both types, among them Qatar Airways. Its Chief Executive, Akbar Al Baker, exasperated that 787 delays meant that he might take deliveries of both types at the same time, asked reporters at a media briefing the rhetorical question, 'Why am I buying two types of airplanes that are doing the same mission?' (Air Transport Intelligence News 2009).

Fleet planning decision criteria are certainly shifting. As points of difference between aircraft models have narrowed, more emphasis is needed on matters that are peripheral to the design or technology level, such as availability, ease of financing and support. From the manufacturers' perspective it is becoming increasingly difficult to offer major step-changes in economic performance with each succeeding design. The newly predominant design criteria embrace the optimisation of the supply chain, reduction in delivery lead times, standardisation of configuration and technology platforms, and the introduction of efficient materials. When it comes to improving existing models the tendency is to focus on incremental benefits that, when accumulated, add up to a surprising amount of improvement over time. For example the introduction of 'Sharklets' on A320 wings from 2012 is expected to yield a fuel-efficiency improvement of at least 3.5 per cent over longer sectors – and this is on an airframe that first saw the light of day 25 years earlier (Airbus 2009b).

The need to rein in carbon emissions, coupled with the threat of permanently high oil prices, has served to heighten customers' appetites for aircraft operating-efficiency improvements. Chipping away gradually with incremental improvements is certainly one way of reaching both efficiency and environmental goals, as well as mitigating exposure to future fuel price rises and maintaining competitive edge. But, at some point along this path of continuous improvement, diminishing returns will set in. The trick is to anticipate the point at which this is likely to happen and plan for a totally new design. A trigger is needed, and that trigger should bring with it the promise of fuel-efficiency improvements of at least 20 per cent, and preferably much more. If not, there is a risk that all the value in a new design would be swallowed up by the next spike in fuel prices.

In the past, designers looked to radical new concepts, such as blended wing-bodied aircraft, to kick-start the new wave of aircraft development. But fanciful designs of this nature ignore the dramatic effect on aircraft handling and airport operations, as well as the effect on the market value of existing designs. Barring a major breakthrough in technology, it seems almost certain that we shall be sticking with the conventional concept of circular fuselage, wing, tail plane and engines mounted either below the wing or at the rear of the fuselage. It is also likely that we will not see a major evolution in aircraft size. Ideas of aircraft carrying thousands of passengers will just not happen because of the economic challenges of maintaining consistently high payloads, integration and handling of such vehicles into airports, and potentially uneconomic turnaround times. However, we might expect new generations of aircraft families to have higher payload capacities than currently.

In fact, the most likely visual change to aircraft design will be delivered by the engine manufacturers, who have been busily conjuring up new technologies that may finally become the long-awaited next step in design.

The Engine is the Key

Engine manufacturers, just like the airframe manufacturers, constantly improve their existing designs through upgrades. Spurred on by the idea that higher fuel prices will be a permanent feature of airline economics in the future, the major engine suppliers have all been readying themselves for fundamentally different designs that will transform both the appearance and the performance of aircraft in the future. The choice boils down to two concepts.

First, we will see the resurrection of an idea that has been around for a long time, but has at last come of age: the geared turbofan engine, which is sometimes referred to as the propfan. Pratt & Whitney has developed its PW1000G PurePower engine family with initial applications on the Mitsubishi regional jet as well as the Bombardier CSeries aircraft. The potential impact of this engine is so radical that it is worth taking a moment to explain the concept. Conventional turbofan engines comprise low- and high-speed turbines driving compressors as well as the fan, which is located on the same shaft. The problem is that the turbine produces its most effective power when turning fast, whereas fans are most efficient when they are large and turn slowly. This is because a lot of slow-moving air generates more efficient thrust than air ejected at high temperature and high pressure from the core. The most fuel-and noise-efficient solution is to continue to increase the fan diameter, which in turn increases the bypass ratio, being the ratio of air that passes around the core as opposed to through the core. As the bypass ratio gets larger, the engine requires more stages in the lower-pressure turbine to drive an increasingly bigger fan. At some point in the design a limit is reached as the increasing weight of the engine leads to a loss in fuel performance. Pratt & Whitney's solution is to use a gearing mechanism that allows the fan to move slowly while enabling the turbine to rotate at its most efficient speed. The effect is an engine with a significantly higher bypass ratio, a fuel burn improvement of 15 per cent over current best engines, and a 75 per cent improvement in noise footprint. Paul Finklestein, Director of Market Development and Sales Strategy, Commercial Engines at Pratt & Whitney says, 'These dramatic results are fundamentally physics based, because a higher bypass ratio means lower fuel and lower fan tip speed means lower noise.' Pratt & Whitney has decided to initially focus on an engine developing thrust ranging from 10,000 to 40,000 pounds, aimed at the single-aisle market, because there has not been a significant evolution of technology in that size category for many years. Says Finklestein, 'We've studied applications up to 115,000 pounds of thrust and we see no limitation on the technical application of geared technology.'

The second conceptual opportunity is an even more dramatic leap of technology: the open rotor engine. Like the geared turbofan, there is nothing new in the idea. Open rotor engines were discussed over 20 years ago but were shelved owing to risk and noise concerns. Nevertheless, open rotor is the development path favoured by the other two major engine suppliers, Rolls-Royce and General Electric. Open rotor technology also involves the use of a gearbox and much larger blades than in an encased turbofan engine. In the open rotor configuration the engine is rather like a turboprop, but with two rows of counter-rotating propellers. With a conventional propeller, air is expelled outwards, but in an open rotor design the air is trapped between the two sets of blades, thus allowing the aircraft to fly faster than a turboprop and more efficiently than a turbofan. As the engine does not have a nacelle or fan casing, the weight and complexities are reduced. Potential fuel savings range from 15 per cent to up to 50 per cent depending on the design, and the degree of compromise that might be needed in operation. For example, you can always squeeze more efficiency by flying at lower altitudes and lower speeds, and by restricting sector lengths and consequently fuel uplift. Open rotor engines will doubtless face certification challenges that are unknown at this point.

All the major engine manufacturers are therefore preparing themselves to offer the airline industry a step-change in aircraft operating economics and, to boot, a big help in reducing carbon emissions. The longer the airframe builders procrastinate about replacing their existing models, the more time the engine companies have to perfect their radical designs.

Who Will Blink First?

Technological advances like the geared turbofan or open rotor will not automatically become the catalyst for manufacturers to launch a totally new aircraft design. That decision is shaped by a series of other considerations, with finance and competitive advantage topping the list. Airbus in particular has suffered dismal financial woes for several years. Failure to deliver the A380 and A400M on time heaped unanticipated financial burdens on the company, which had to navigate a tough passage of cost overruns and late delivery penalty payments to customers. Total A380 costs were pushed from the original US$12 billion to around US$18 billion (Rothman 2009). Heaped on top of those problems was the need to introduce internal cost reductions, plus the fall-out from the economic downturn, where the financing shortfall in 2009 was estimated to be as high as US$20 billion (Rothman 2008). A350 development costs have ballooned from US$5.3 billion in 2005 to over US$13 billion in 2009 (*Flug Revue* 2005; Reuters 2009), so it is hardly surprising that the appetite to shoulder even more costs to support an A320 family replacement would wear thin, particularly when demand for the current aircraft is still strong. Speaking at the press launch of the *Global Market Forecast* in September 2009, Airbus's Chief Commercial Officer John Leahy indicated that an A320 replacement will not see the light of day before 2024. Boeing is likewise seemingly in no hurry to rush into a completely new 737 family aircraft. Its most logical path would be to channel 787 technologies and production techniques onto its next single-aisle product.

The 20-year forecasts of both Airbus and Boeing indicate a huge market for aircraft in the single-aisle category. Airbus believes that the demand will be for 16,977 units, valued at US$1,206 billion, and Boeing puts the numbers at 19,460 units and US$1,420 billion (Airbus 2009a; Boeing 2009). It is hardly surprising that the airframe makers are busily studying totally new designs to meet this demand. The A320 replacement project, called the NSR, or New Short-Range aircraft, and Boeing's 737RS, or Replacement Study, have been public knowledge since 2006 (Norris 2006). With similar engine technology likely to be available to either manufacturer, they will be seeing the airframe design as being the ultimate discriminator. Twenty years ago Airbus achieved some success with a fuselage cross-section that was more attractive than Boeing's, but the single-aisle aircraft of the future may yet turn out to be much more of a commodity offering.

Not everybody is happy with the idea that new single-aisle aircraft may not see the light of day until 2024. Chris Schroeder, Head of Corporate Social Responsibility, Environment and Fuel Optimisation at Qatar Airways says, 'Boeing and Airbus have made a huge mistake here, there is no doubt about it. The call is for a brand new design, and we definitely don't welcome this [date of 2024].' Qatar Airways is positioning itself as a leader in technology and, in particular, is supporting environmental initiatives to restrict carbon emissions and promote alternative fuels, as we shall see in Chapter 7. It is not just technology leaders who are likely to be concerned about Airbus and Boeing putting the brakes on a totally new aircraft design. Many US airlines are saddled with large fleets of elderly MD-80s and 737s. Consequently, they will be making increasingly large commitments to the current single-aisle offerings which they will need to live with for an extended period of time. Says Schroeder, 'Buying an aircraft is a long-term commitment. Airlines replacing MD-80s with a huge A320 fleet will be stuck with old technology until the manufacturers finally come up with updated versions.'

Boeing's Randy Tinseth was unapologetic when I suggested to him that he might be putting off the launch of single-aisle replacement aircraft for parochial commercial considerations. 'I think it's a little bit unfair,' he said, in measured, polite tones. 'Our customers want an airplane that would be 15 per cent better than today's 737 in terms of fuel efficiency, and 25 or 30 per cent less expensive to maintain. I will tell you that the technologies to create that airplane don't exist today. The technology for the engine, the materials, the systems or the aerodynamics isn't there.' Christian Scherer, Airbus's Head of Strategy, completely agrees. 'History proves that successful aircraft have to bring a significant step-change in operating efficiency – say 15 to 20 per cent. Today, no-one in aerospace has technologies to make that step-change.'

The decision by the major manufacturers to delay all-new aircraft designs is not popular and does not remove pressures from airlines for more efficiency development. Apart from a continuous need to reduce operating costs, the industry also has obligations to control carbon emissions. Re-engine programmes could yet be a way of keeping the wolves at bay until the time is right to take the plunge with all-new designs. However, it is not clear whether the radical new engine configurations under development can be practically accommodated under the wing of the 737, due to ground clearance.

There is no doubting that the single-aisle replacement issue is a high-stakes game. Says Boeing's Tinseth, 'The last thing you want to do is bring a new airplane to the market, and then some new disrupting technology enters the marketplace and obsoletes your product. So we're going to be very careful, very thoughtful and very measured.' But procrastination is unpopular with aircraft buyers. If either Airbus or Boeing misplay their cards, then a wave of competitors is itching to grab a slice of the single-aisle pie.

The New Pretenders

In my time at Airbus I was frequently struck by the way in which the company summarily dismissed the potential market incursion of the 100-plus seat market by regional jets. Once in a while there would be an internal appraisal of the regional jet market, which would be mulled over for a while before we filed the reports and turned our attention once more to the big stuff. It is true that historically there had been relatively little overlap between the top end of the regional jet market and the bottom end of the Airbus and Boeing product lines. Boeing's foray at the lower end was limited to the 717, inherited from McDonnell-Douglas as the MD-95. Airbus toyed with regional jet-sized A316 and A317 concepts for a while and ended up producing a double-shrink of the A320 called the A318, which has a disappointing sales record. However, Embraer and Bombardier have been nibbling at the heels of the 100-plus seat market with aircraft styled on the popular family approach. It is early days for the Bombardier CSeries, but Lufthansa's order for the type may yet prove to be a catalyst for other significant carriers to follow.

It is easy to see why the regional jet manufacturers are attracted to the 100-plus seat market. Increasing fuel prices have rendered the 30- to 50-seater jets obsolete. This means that the manufacturers have been forced to turn their attention to improving their turboprop designs as well as investing in larger-gauge aircraft. So the regional jet market is poised to become increasingly crowded with new products from Embraer and Bombardier and from new players in China, Korea, Russia and Japan. Companies from emerging economies have been supplying components to Boeing and Airbus for many years, but the time is fast approaching for these countries to make that giant leap and produce whole airframes themselves. Growth of engineering know-how, technical skills and production capabilities has become more pervasive. The new breed of supplier has a goal of reaching beyond their respective home markets. The Japanese Mitsubishi Regional Jet, or MRJ, has already broken through the perception barrier, having secured credible orders from Trans States Holdings in the United States, as well as All Nippon Airways in Japan. What is particularly significant is that two of these aircraft types, the CSeries and the MRJ, will be powered by the Pratt & Whitney PW1000G PurePower geared turbofan. The Chinese manufacturer Comac (China Aircraft Corporation of China) is planning to fly its CFM Leap-X powered C919, which will be configured with between 130 and 200 seats, by around 2017. Comac is forecasting deliveries of 2,000 aircraft over a 20-year period (CFM 2009). But the smaller ARJ-21 has suffered delays during its eight-year gestation and still awaits all-important certification from the US Federal Aviation Administration.

Will the new regional jets succeed? As they are mostly supported by governments and national interests you would think that the outlook is rosy. However, all of the new models are programmed to appear in the latter part of the current decade, and that means the new aircraft will be based on current technologies, with the exception of the engine in some cases. So here is one more reason why neither Airbus nor Boeing has a huge appetite to invest too early in totally new aircraft. Competition from the regional end of the market will not be dangerous enough because none of these aircraft will have made the step-change that the airlines are looking for. Rather more worrying for the new regional manufacturers is that by the time the all-new Airbus and Boeing products enter the market, the next wave of regional jets will hardly be mature, let alone profitable.

One report has evaluated the impact that the new entrants could have on the 100- to 210-seat market should they all achieve their goals. The surprising conclusion is that Boeing and Airbus's current market share of 88 per cent in this segment could shrink to as little as 40 per cent (King 2009). However, this is rather unlikely to come to pass for a number of reasons. First, many existing customers would probably need technical compatibility with other aircraft produced by Boeing and Airbus, and this militates against new designs with no broad family of products. Second, it is too much to expect that significant numbers of airlines would completely roll over their fleets into the new types. Third, experience suggests that it takes decades to establish global support structures and, fourth, the incumbents are hardly going to be standing still, watching their tight grip on the market loosened.

In Conclusion

Aircraft designers and producers are the most motivated, energetic and optimistic people I have ever met in the aerospace business. They have been lauded as brilliant and visionary engineers. Aircraft sales teams are relentlessly driven to place their products with customers and have achieved astounding success. At the same time, the manufacturers have been labelled parochial, arrogant and self-centred. Yet their product strategies have shaped today's airline business and will doubtless continue to do so. We should thank them. But can the industry rely on their forecasts? Airbus and Boeing are doggedly sticking to their own respective views concerning the long-term need for very large aircraft and both vigorously deny that market opinions are influenced by the legacy of product decisions that have set them both on different paths.

Unsurprisingly, the airline industry is more preoccupied with the short term. Against expectations, the aircraft makers successfully delivered their intended production in 2009 and remain unapologetic over accusations that they are fuelling the airlines with capacity they do not really need. New aircraft can pay for themselves very quickly, they argue, due to fuel burn advantages over earlier-generation technology. This may be the case, but it is nevertheless extraordinary that an industry brought to its knees in 2009 by crippling economic crisis can so easily absorb just shy of 1,000 new aircraft. Readily available financing and loan guarantees, often using the aircraft themselves as security, smooth the path.

The decisions by Airbus and Boeing on the replacement of their highly successful A320 and 737 families are the most fundamental the manufacturers have ever faced. A miscue by either company, either in terms of timing or technology, could prove disastrous. The regional jet manufacturers, especially the new entrants, are lining up to grab what they may consider a long overdue rightful share of the market dominated by the 'big two'. Yet questions remain over whether the new regional jets will be competitive in the longer term when new Airbus and Boeing products finally arrive. There is no doubt that the single-aisle market is poised to become the greatest battlefield of all time.

References

Airbus, 2009a. *Global Market Forecast 2009–2028*. Available at: http://www.airbus.com/en/corporate/gmf/ (accessed 20 December 2009).

Airbus, 2009b. 'Airbus Launches "Sharklet" Large Wingtip Devices for A320 Family with Commitment from Air New Zealand'. 15 November Available at: http://www.airbus.com/en/presscentre/pressreleases/press-release/?tx_ttnews%5BpS%5D=1273418413&tx_ttnews%5Bpointer%5D=10&tx_ttnews%5Btt_news%5D=2027&tx_ttnews%5BbackPid%5D=1683&cHash=4f866b0987 (accessed 21 May 2010).

Air Transport Intelligence News, 2009. 'Boeing Rescues Qatar Airways 787 Deal'. 30 July. Available at: http://www.flightglobal.com/articles/2009/07/30/330380/boeing-rescues-qatar-airways-787-deal.html (accessed 29 December 2009).

Boeing, 2009. 'Current Market Outlook 2009–2028'. Available at: http://www. boeing.com/commercial/cmo/index.html (accessed 15 December 2009).

CFM, 2009. 'Advanced LEAP-X1C Engine Chosen as Sole Powerplant to Launch New COMAC C919 Aircraft'. 21 December. Available at: http:// www.cfm56.com/press/news/advanced+leap-x1c+engine+chosen+as+s ole+powerplant+to+launch+new+comac+c919+aircraft/513 (accessed 21 December 2009).

Flug Revue, 2005. 'Paris Air Show June 2005'. Available at: http://www.flug-revue.rotor.com/FRTypen/FRA350.htm (accessed 1 December 2009).

Gates, D., 2009. 'Money's Short to Pay for New Boeing, Airbus Jets, Experts Warn'. 18 March. Available at: http://seattletimes.nwsource.com/html/ boeingaerospace/2008877997_istat18.html (accessed 18 December 2009).

King, M., 2009. 'Airbus and Boeing Currently Have about an 88% Market Share in the 100- to 200-Seat Single Aisle Market Segment'. 17 November. Available at: http://www.pr-inside.com/airbus-and-boeing-currently-have-about-r1587099.htm (accessed 10 December 2009).

Norris, G., 2006. 'The 737 Story: Smoke and Mirrors Obscure 737 and Airbus A320 Replacement Studies'. 7 February. Available at: http://www. flightglobal.com/articles/2006/02/07/204506/the-737-story-smoke-and-mirrors-obscure-737-and-airbus-a320-replacement.html (accessed 8 December 2009).

Ostrower, J., 2009. 'Spirit Aerosystems "Terribly Worried" about 737 Production Rates'. 6 November. Available at: http://www.flightglobal. com/articles/2009/11/06/334477/spirit_aerosystems-terribly-worried-about-737-production-rates.html (accessed 18 December 2009).

Reuters, 2009. 'Airbus Says A350 Project to Cost 11 Billion Euro'. 16 June. Available at: http://uk.reuters.com/article/idUKTRE55F1Y720090616 (accessed 5 December 2009).

Rothman, A., 2008. 'Airbus Says It Has "Leeway" to Finance Airlines'. 25 November. Available at: http://www.seattlepi.com/business/389285_ airbus25.html (accessed 19 December 2009).

Rothman, A., 2009. 'Airbus Cuts Planned A380 Deliveries on Deferrals (Update 2)'. 6 May. Available at: http://www.bloomberg.com/apps/news ?pid=newsarchive&sid=aBJt_.cAg1uc (accessed 17 December 2009).

Rothman, A. and Ray, S., 2009. 'Airbus, Boeing Duel to Save Jet Orders as Airlines Park Planes'. 11 June. Available at: http://www.bloomberg.com/ apps/news?pid=20601109&sid=aXMajoxkj.CQ (accessed 10 December 2009).

Sobie, B., 2009. 'IATA's Bisignani Predicts Massive 2009 Delivery Shortfall for Airbus and Boeing'. 20 February. Available at: http://www.flightglobal. com/articles/2009.02/20/322852/iatas_bisignani-predicts-massive-2009-delivery-shortfall-for-airbus-and.html (accessed 13 December 2009).

Thomas, W., 1928. 'The Thomas Theorem'. Available at: http://en.wikipedia. org/wiki/Thomas_theorem (accessed 10 December 2009).

Wallace, J., 2007. 'Airbus All In On Need for Jumbo – But Boeing Still Doubtful'. 24 November. Available at: http://www.seattlepi.com/business/336611_airbus24.html (accessed 15 December 2009).

Chapter 3

'Love Me Do': The Changing Nature of Traveller Expectations

Around ten years ago my wife Judith and I arrived at an almost deserted Air France check-in at JFK airport in New York, ready to board a Concorde flight to Paris. One hour before departure, the complement of around 50 passengers tucked into a light breakfast in the dedicated lounge. The meal was meagre but served up with customary French chic. The flight itself was calm, noticeably swift so far as flight-time over the Atlantic was concerned, but otherwise uneventful. The cabin crew were quietly efficient, the seat comfort was adequate rather than exceptional and the in-flight meal was, naturally, exquisite.

But our journey that day did not end in Paris. We were booked onward from Paris to Toulouse, and it was at this point that the travel experience abruptly altered. The first challenge was to make the transfer from Charles de Gaulle to Orly airport. We elected to squash ourselves into the Air France transfer bus for just over an hour. Then we steeled ourselves for the true ordeal of the day; struggling with all our might through a loathsome Orly check-in and security procedure along with a mass of disgruntled fellow travellers. Assailed by the peculiar odour that seems to hover permanently within Orly airport, we shuffled with the crowd through the claustrophobic boarding gate, stood queuing in the sweltering jetway and finally squeezed into our seats on the crowded A320 for the one-hour flight to our destination. The in-flight service was indifferent, the seat pitch cramped, the aircraft departed and arrived late and, to crown the experience, Air France succeeded in losing my wife's suitcase which, to this day, has never been found. So, after a pampered and relaxing transatlantic crossing in civil aviation's greatest technical triumph, we emerged from Toulouse Blagnac airport exhausted and bad-tempered. For days afterwards, all we could think about was that last awful domestic connection and the whereabouts of the lost suitcase. The pleasant glow from the Dom Pérignon had long faded.

Now I have a confession to make. Instead of paying the usual fare of just over US$8,000 each for our flights, we had been guests of Air France. Like most road warriors, I had amassed a large collection of unspent frequent flyer miles and, at the behest of Air France, gladly accepted their offer to clear the account through a weekend Concorde experience to New York. The flight may have been a reward but it had nevertheless been earned by several years' loyalty towards Air France. So, in a sense, I felt that I had paid my dues. However, had I paid hard cash for the privilege of sampling the airline's flagship service I would have probably been even more mortified by the Paris to Toulouse experience.

In all honesty, the connecting flight was not that bad. What made it *seem* bad was the heightened expectation that I had irrationally developed as a result of my status of being a Concorde client for the day. I had witnessed the two extremes of the air travel experience spectrum back-to-back and formed an unfair opinion of the less satisfying of the two. There are certainly some lessons to be learned from the example.

First, failure to anticipate and act upon passenger expectations can alienate previously loyal customers. Second, the new breed of low-cost airline has permanently modified travellers' expectations in the markets they serve. Third, the world of air travel is becoming increasingly commoditised, with implications on customer expectations and product design. The remainder of this chapter will explore these issues.

The Complexities of Passenger Expectations

Every passenger has an individual basket of expectations of a service for which they are about to experience. These may be conscious or subconscious, and may vary according to geography, culture, nationality, journey purpose, overall journey length, gender, age, degree of infirmity, position in the social scale, socio-economic status, and the demographic cohort to which a passenger may belong.

Synovate, a leading global market research company, has conducted a wide-ranging analysis of air travel expectations that embraces many of the variables described above (Synovate 2008). In 2008 the organisation surveyed 6,900 air travellers in markets covering the Americas, Europe, the Middle East, the Gulf region and Asia. In the survey, passengers were asked to state the key thing that they liked most about air travel. One of the attributes the respondents could choose was 'It's fast and it gets me to where I need to be quickly'. The majority of people, 56 per cent, chose this response and, significantly, the highest score for this attribute came from the United States, with a score of 84 per cent. That result would seem to deliver a clear message. Americans just want to get from A to B as rapidly and painlessly as possible. In a country where air travel takes place on such a huge scale and is so critical to the nation's well-being it is a logical result. Synovate classifies this particular type of travel as purely transactional.

However, at the other end of the scale, 42 per cent of Egyptians rate 'being served' as their favourite feature of air travel. In the Egyptian culture, air travel is considered as a prestigious activity, rather than a strict necessity, so passengers expect traditional Arabic hospitality and respect. Egyptair recognises this in its corporate vision, which is to 'deliver competitive customer service with true Egyptian spirit'. We might refer to this type of travel as gratuitously pampered.

Building an understanding of where market expectations lie is an essential part of any airline commercial strategy and pretty obvious. But it is too simplistic to imagine that all customers fall either into the transactional side of the spectrum or else into the gratuitously pampered side. So, airlines pursuing a highly diverse market, in terms of network breadth, culture, journey purpose and so on, are clearly faced with a more complex product and service design task than airlines that focus on a particular market segment or else operate a simple network. Hence, the marketing challenge for low-cost carriers is somewhat more straightforward.

To revert to my own experience in flying from New York to Toulouse, it is clear that Air France has a significantly greater challenge in managing a complex set of passenger expectations shaped by its multifaceted network and market. The potential for confusion and misinterpretation of passenger service delivery is consequently high. To further complicate matters, coupling airline networks together with alliance or code-share partners amplifies the challenge. My lasting impression of what should have been a memorable journey on Air France's most prestigious flight was soured by a domestic travel experience that, under other circumstances, might have passed for 'adequate'. The close juxtaposition of two experiences muddled perception and created the feeling of failed expectation. I was hardly gratuitously pampered in my Paris to Toulouse shuttle. If I am honest, it felt more like being gratuitously abused.

The Legacy of Low Cost

We owe the low-cost carriers a lot. Not only have they forced change upon the air travel market by creating opportunities for people to fly more affordably, they have radically changed the landscape of airline economics. Unit costs have tumbled, new mini-profit centres have been created which other airlines were treating as a cost, and operating efficiency has dramatically improved. As a consequence of the initiatives and innovations thrust upon the market by the low-cost sector, all airlines have been driven to implement cost improvement programmes, just to stay competitive. In fact, airlines have to create and sustain a permanent momentum and culture for change just in order to keep pace. Bravo to the low-cost airlines. Why did it happen all of a sudden? Well, it did not.

The so-called low-cost 'revolution' is really a fallacy. The phenomenon can be more correctly described as the low-cost 'slow-burning fuse'. The first wave of low-cost carriers pre-dates the most well known of today's airlines by a long way. This wave comprised a collection of low-cost and low-fare carriers, in particular Southwest Airlines, augmented by some visionary experiments such as the Laker Airways 'Skytrain' service across the North Atlantic with its walk-up low fares, and People Express, a US carrier for everyman but ultimately crushed by the weight of the old order. The second wave is epitomised by the likes of

Ryanair, easyJet, AirAsia, Air Berlin and dozens upon dozens of lookalikes. It is this second wave that can claim to have changed the air travel landscape in a radical manner. The third wave is really a phase in which the edges of the low-cost model have become significantly blurred. For example, Kingfisher Airlines in India was initially perceived by many to be a low-cost carrier. In fact, Airbus persisted in listing Kingfisher as a low-cost carrier in its marketing messages for several years. However, this could not be further from reality. Kingfisher prides itself in offering a quality product and service. It would be a mistake to confuse its funky image with the stereotype of the breed. Also, some airlines that were initially pigeon-holed as low-cost, such as JetBlue Airways, have gradually moved in the direction of a full-service carrier. Well-known JetBlue product attributes such as leather seats and live television typify this trend. At the same time, full-service carriers have been drawn into the low-cost ambit in order to shore up their market. Aer Lingus pulled off a transformation into a 'lower-cost' carrier by emulating as many of the low-cost features as it could, such as fleet commonality with standard and high seating configuration, short turn times at airports and high utilisation.

The consequence of these strategic changes is that commercial battle lines have become confused. The convergence of the models has eroded the purity of the original low-cost model. Gradually, succinctly, and almost by stealth, every airline has become something of a low-cost carrier. This is not strictly true across the board, but is certainly broadly true in short- to medium-haul markets where low-cost carriers have mostly taken root. Long-haul markets are not totally immune from the effect but do tend to operate to different rules, as we shall see later in this chapter.

Changes wrought in the second wave of the low-cost 'slow-burning fuse' have presented many new challenges, among them the problem of identifying the changing expectations of the market. At one stage in the transformation, low-cost carriers started charging for in-flight drinks and snacks, and this brought about something of a knee-jerk reaction from some of the traditional airlines. I well remember taking an intra-European flight on SWISS, very soon after its introduction of a policy of charging for hot beverages. My business-class tariff was just over €1,000 for a return flight of just under two hours yet I, along with my fellow travellers, was asked to pay for coffee. Doubtless, SWISS felt that it was keeping pace with the new trend of turning in-flight catering into a profit centre of its own. Mutterings of disapproval were heard throughout the cabin and, emboldened by the feeling of shared indignation, mutterings soon rose to something of a crescendo, much to the embarrassment of the cabin crew. It was all rather un-SWISS. The general feeling was that the act of charging for coffee was unprincipled and petty. Had these same passengers been travelling on rival easyJet I am sure that not a murmur would have been heard. Airlines perceived as being low-cost are more easily forgiven for audacity than airlines sporting a nation's flag. Sensing a revolt, traditional airlines quickly abandoned the idea of charging their premium passengers for their coffee, and, at the same time, low-cost airlines began to offer snacks and beverages free of charge. And so we have another example of the levelling of the airline product playing field.

The true dilemma for airlines is to understand what parameters drive a customer's choice of carrier. The answer is wrapped up in another enigma, which is how to build an understanding of the perception of a charged service, especially one that had previously been offered free of charge. And this is the crux of the matter. The low-cost carriers have succeeded in creating a completely new perception of what air travel is all about. They have not had to focus so much on changing existing preconceptions to the same degree as the traditional carriers because so much of their market has been relatively new. The onus is therefore more on the traditional airlines to re-educate the market.

What is clear is that airline choice is driven to a greater degree than ever by value for money. This is an inevitable consequence of the completion of the transition of air travel from being perceived as a luxury for the elite to being a true mass-market commodity. Couple this trend with the economic pressures brought about by recession and a new cocktail has been mixed. The industry is at a stage where a focus on low cost and competitive pricing is all-embracing and the days of needless and wasteful investment in product quality to garner market share are dead and buried. However, not all markets have succumbed to this trend. Long-haul, high-yield, business-driven markets are still influenced by high product quality and are likely to remain so.

Airports, it is fair to point out, see traveller expectations in a different way. Daniel Sallier is an air transport specialist with airport forecasting experience. 'Passenger populations have different expectations and sensitivities ranging from "red" – the more demanding ones – to "green", the less demanding ones. Occasional travellers on leisure trips are the easiest to deal with, even in situations of severe disruption, as long as they are kept informed. On the other hand, frequent travellers on business trips are more demanding. This is why you have fast-track systems, dedicated check-in desks, parking lots and even dedicated terminals.' Importantly, the fall in premium demand is hardly noticed by airports as commercial revenues are not significantly different between the various market segments. Nevertheless, Sallier suspects that the high-end tax-free boutiques may feel the pinch.

A wedge is being driven between two extremes. Travel markets are being polarised into short-haul, price-driven, value-for-money routes on the one hand, and long-haul, quality-driven product for long-haul on the other. Perhaps the middle ground of the future is only available as a niche business for a small number of long-haul low-cost wannabes.

Whatever strategy is adopted, an airline, like any other business, creates and influences market perception through its brand.

The Touchy-Feely Stuff

In my regular seminars for airline middle and senior managers I often launch a discussion on airline branding by displaying on a screen a procession of partially concealed airline logos, inviting the audience to call out the identities of the airlines. In practically every case, the appearance of the Ryanair 'harp' tailfin would result in silence descending upon the room. The irony is that, just one hour earlier, these managers would have been earnestly debating the huge impact that Ryanair has made on the airline industry. Clearly there is a difference between visual imagery and the depth of brand awareness.

On the other hand, the smallest detail of an airline logo has the potential to create uproar. The new Brussels Airlines, formed in 2007 from the merger of SN Brussels Airlines and Virgin Express, chose a design where the 'B' of Brussels was composed of a series of red dots. Nobody in the airline paid particular attention to the number of red dots used to make up the letter 'B'. When the passengers saw the logo they quickly realised that the logo designer had chosen 13 dots, certain to bring bad luck to superstitious travellers! A flood of complaints forced Brussels Airlines to make amends by adding a fourteenth dot (Casert 2007).

Perhaps the most vociferous market reaction to an airline logo can be traced back to 1997 when British Airways introduced a variety of so-called ethnic tailfin designs in an effort to convey the idea that the airline was cosmopolitan in attitude, rather than too focused on dark-suited businessmen. When Prime Minister Margaret Thatcher expressed her disapproval by draping a handkerchief over an aircraft model sporting the new concept, and in full view of the world's media, British Airways was quickly ridiculed and criticised for being out of touch. It was not only the customers who revolted against the ethnic fins; ground controllers complained that they had difficulty identifying aircraft when giving taxiing instructions. British Airways had already invested £60 million in the new colour scheme but had no choice but to revert to the sanctuary of the traditional Union flag to appease its critics.

Even in the somewhat conservative world of aircraft type branding, Airbus cleverly rebranded the A3XX as the A380 (rather than A350, being the next available number in the series at that time) in order to flatter Asian airline buyers, and Singapore Airlines in particular. The number '8' is, of course, an auspicious number in Asian culture.

Oh Brand, Wherefore Art Thou?

With all the attention given to airline branding and the depth of feeling shown by aircraft buyers, passengers, industry watchers and workers alike, one would expect to see airline brands standing shoulder to shoulder with the world's most recognisable and elegant brands. After all, airlines are glamorous, symbolise national pride, and represent high technical ideals. However, this is quite wrong. The myth ends here.

The sad fact is that not a single airline is represented in the regular surveys of the top 100 'most powerful' global brands (Interbrand 2009). Most lists of this type focus on brand value as opposed to brand influence, so the airline business is hardly likely to compete on value terms with the likes of Google, Nokia, Microsoft and Wal-Mart. However, if we focus on surveys that embrace opinion on whether a brand *influences* behaviour, then airlines do actually creep into the picture. On this basis the global picture is still bereft of airlines but, at a regional level, six Asian airlines crept into the top 40, with Air Asia grabbing the highest position at number 6 (see Figure 3.1).

1	Sony	11	Proton
2	Toyota	12	Star TV
3	HSBC	13	**Cathay Pacific**
4	Samsung	14	Hello Kitty
5	Honda	15	Acer
6	**Air Asia**	16	Hyundai
7	Globe Telecom	17	Nissan
8	LG Electronics	18	Mitsubishi
9	Lonely Planet	19	Nintendo
10	**Singapore Airlines**	20	Tiger Beer
21	Tata	31	nudie drinks
22	Mazda	32	Barista
23	Lenovo	33	Rip Curl
24	Mandarin Oriental Group	34	Muji
25	Infosys	35	Baidu
26	**Jet Airways**	36	Bank of China
27	**Jetstar**	37	SingTel
28	**Qantas**	38	Carlton Draught
29	JobStreet.com	39	Daewoo
30	Peninsula Hotels	40	Banyan Tree

Figure 3.1   Recognisable brands in Asia

Source: Brandchannel (2006).

The challenge to develop a valuable and enduring airline brand has become particularly difficult as air travel becomes commoditised. The tendency for travel choice to become increasingly driven by price rather than product design, or even quality, is likely to continue as long as difficult economic conditions prevail. Indeed, it is arguable that reversion to the days of unabashed quality in the skies with little regard for price is just not going to happen, except in hotly contested high-yield or niche markets. Business owners require their employees to behave with more attention to their travel budget than in the past. As earlier-generation product differentiators cancel each other out or else diminish in importance, brand becomes a significantly more important choice determinant. Having a great product or great level of service can no longer be considered sufficient to build a market. Airlines must work harder to breed loyalty, capture new business and, especially, divert business from a competitor. As buyers increase their focus on price, they correspondingly reduce their focus on the more traditional product differentiators. Interestingly, some of the most recognisable airlines have capitalised on the cult of personality for their success.

Hero Worship

Throughout the history of civil aviation, along with many other industries and types of business, there have been many personalities and brands that have become seemingly untouchable, in the sense that they appear beyond criticism or censure. Some obvious ones that spring to mind are Virgin Atlantic Airways and Southwest Airlines. Either through lucky timing, ruthlessness, obstinacy, uniqueness, personality or a blend of several of these business 'attributes', these untouchables have carved a strong niche for themselves and endeared themselves to the public at large and, critically, to the press. Mostly, the success of these airlines has been propelled by a charismatic leader who can emit such an aura that the masses literally flock to their feet in admiration and mutual approbation. I do not mean to sound cynical.

One of the brightest and most deserved successes is Virgin Atlantic Airways. The all-pervasive brand has just the right amount of punch and irreverence to capture the imagination of a broad spectrum of social groups and demographic cohorts. And Sir Richard Branson exudes just the right amount of humbled charm to keep the press sweet and the Virgin brand at the forefront of many of the industries where he has a presence. The strong brand values of Virgin – in particular, customer attentiveness and service quality – seem to automatically attach themselves to new ventures without any great effort. This is beautifully illustrated in a four-minute interview given by Sir Richard on the G4TV cable and satellite channel in which he promoted Virgin America. The station formerly specialised in video gaming and was once known for having the smallest audience of any US cable network. That Branson agreed to the interview in the first place was something of a masterstroke and one can presume that he was fully aware of the potential for viral transmission whereby content, in this case in the form of a recorded interview, has the potential to be rapidly daisy-chained through the Internet. We shall examine this effect in more detail in Chapter 6. Thus, Sir Richard's rather lightweight interview with Chris Hardwick of G4TV was well executed, as the style of the programme seemed to snap into place with Virgin's image. Ironically, in the interview Sir Richard honestly claimed to have had little to do with the conception of Virgin America, but the hypercharged interviewer conveniently glossed over that point and gushed so enthusiastically about the airline that the viewer was left in no doubt that Virgin America provides the best customer experience in the industry. As well as charming his interviewer on G4TV, Branson's infectious enthusiasm rubs off on to his staff, and this feeds directly through to the end customer. It is not an exaggeration to say that Branson has single-handedly put some glamour back into flying (Hardwick 2009).

One critical aspect of the success of the Virgin brand has been the decision to associate the brand with laudable initiatives that capture the public's imagination. As an example, the Virgin Earth Challenge is financing a US$25 million prize to whoever can come up with the best idea for removing greenhouse gases and reducing global warming. Another savvy move was to climb on the bandwagon of the unexpected success of the former Brawn GP team in the 2009 Formula One championship. Virgin is by no means the first airline to jump on to the Formula One bandwagon, but Sir Richard lost no time in getting the Virgin insignia on the Brawn cars and making sure that he would be seen by vast television audiences sashaying along the pit lane. Emboldened by racetrack success, Virgin quickly moved to establish its own team, Virgin Racing, for the 2010 Formula One season.

However, another airline personality with big ambition, the ebullient Dr Vijay Mallya, was initially somewhat less successful with his own foray into the seductive world of Formula One. Dr Mallya's Kingfisher Airlines has certainly made a mark on the Indian stage, but on the somewhat more cynical global stage of Formula One we became accustomed to seeing Mallya's Force India team finish consistently at the back of the field in the 2008 season. However, persistence paid off, and Dr Mallya must certainly have been as surprised as everyone else when Force India's performance was suddenly transformed towards the end of the 2009 Formula One season. The magnetism of racing has also attracted AirAsia's Tony Fernandes, who is behind the resurrection of the Lotus brand in the sport.

Picking winners at the race track is one thing, but projecting a continually successful public profile is another. Even Sir Richard has been known to falter. Dressing up as an ordinary rail worker to publicise Virgin's UK rail operation attracted criticism that he was stereotyping his employees. His public and fans conveniently overlooked the indiscretion (BBC 2009).

The power of the Virgin brand or the public's image of Sir Richard cannot alone account for the success of Virgin Atlantic Airways. The airline has pursued a sensible and consistent strategy and philosophy that have paid off handsomely. There are numerous reasons for this. The business model is not highly dependent on connecting traffic, thereby avoiding complexity and cost. The route structure is composed almost entirely of long-haul routes, thereby extracting the best operating economics out of the aircraft; Virgin Atlantic is a much smaller airline than its customers often suppose, but thanks to the boss's public profile and consistent execution of strategy, generates a lot of attention despite being a relative minnow in the business. Indeed, it has to be admitted that Virgin Atlantic does a lot of things absolutely right.

Another airline with a powerful brand, even though their logo is somewhat low-key, is Ryanair, which has adopted a very different approach to achieve its success. Like Virgin, Ryanair has been led by a charismatic leader, in the form of Michael O'Leary. Sir Richard's swashbuckling spats with his competition have been somewhat genteel compared to those of O'Leary, who comes out of his corner with a good deal more venom. There is no doubt that O'Leary's personal style, abrasive as it is, has been integral to the Ryanair phenomenon. I suspect that many of his detractors secretly admire his razor wit and zany antics. After all, how many other airline chief executive officers would unashamedly accuse the European Commission of being the 'evil empire' and get away with it so easily? Michael O'Leary may have a confrontational style but he also has an honest and strong determination to provide travellers with the lowest fares. That simple message is the one that Ryanair's customers understand. The airline promises very little else and, indeed, is capable of heaping abuse on passengers who have the temerity to actually complain about customer service. For an airline as successful as Ryanair, this matters little. The airline has courted controversy over its cavalier approach to the disabled and has been censured for what some consider an abrasive approach to advertising. Yet Ryanair has managed to tame its market by the simple expedient of limiting, rather than creating, expectation. You get exactly what you pay for and what you expect, and nothing more.

Whereas many major network airlines wrestle with diametrically opposite expectations within their total customer bases, Virgin Atlantic and Ryanair are freed from that challenge thanks to their strong strategic focus, each very different but each perfectly tuned to, and understood by, their respective markets.

Whither the Golden Age?

The onslaught of low-cost airlines in an increasingly price-conscious world has resulted in a more forgiving product feature environment in many short-haul markets. Network carriers have been forced to adopt some of the strategies of the low-cost airlines just to remain competitive. This has doubtless ushered in new, more cost-conscious philosophies in these airlines. The initial success achieved by Aer Lingus in its transformation into a 'lower-cost' carrier bears this out. The big question is whether or not a similar change of philosophy is due in some longer-haul markets.

Historically, 'long-haul' and 'low-cost' have been poor bedfellows. The demise of Oasis Hong Kong in 2008 encapsulated many of the problems of this type of business model. The airline was launched in October 2006, firstly serving London Gatwick, and later adding Vancouver. Initially, the airline offered one-way flights from London to Hong Kong for only £75, a clearly unsustainable fare, but one that created the impression that the glory days of Sir Freddie Laker's Skytrain were returning. Generally, average fares were around half of those of the competition.

A classic confusion between 'low fare' and 'low cost' developed. Oasis Hong Kong leased and operated up to five 747 aircraft, some of which were almost 20 years old, compromising operating efficiency. The aircraft were powered by a mixture of Pratt & Whitney and General Electric engines and had different seating configurations. This complicates maintenance and both the reservations and seat allocation procedures. The airline offered free meals and free drinks in business class. Every passenger had access to a personal television screen, and free headphones, pillows and blankets were available. The economy-class seat pitch was more generous than that of either Virgin Atlantic Airways or British Airways. Such product features were entirely laudable, and even expected on long-haul airlines, but not at half the ticket price!

There was no doubting the popularity of Oasis Hong Kong. The airline carried off a raft of industry accolades such as 'World's Leading New Airline', 'Asia's Leading Budget/No Frill Airline' and 'New Airline of the Year'. At the World Low Cost Airline Congress Awards in 2007 Oasis Hong Kong was voted 'Best Business Carrier' as well as 'Best New Service'. However, picking up industry awards was never likely to shield the airline from the realities of a dubious business strategy and worsening economic conditions.

Crisis turned to catastrophe when fuel prices began to soar in 2008. Losses accumulated to a level of more than HK$1 billion (US$128 million), and the company had no option but to cease operations in April 2008. It is easy to be wise after the event, but it was always going to be a tall order to break into a market that was tightly controlled by a clutch of existing, well-established carriers with substantial networks and access to the routes of their alliance partners. The absence of feed traffic at each end of the routes was a critical stumbling block that Oasis Hong Kong could never address.

Once again, the concept of long-haul low-cost was called into question. Perhaps the failure of Oasis Hong Kong simply reaffirms that the network carriers have got it right after all and that any attempt to break the model is doomed. The baton has been passed to AirAsia X, the latest airline tempted into these dangerous waters, to prove detractors wrong with its operation from Kuala Lumpur to destinations in Australia and to London. The airline's affiliation with the Virgin Group might mean that some of Sir Richard Branson's legendary Midas touch may rub off. More likely, AirAsia's already formidable success in the regional market will leave the long-haul business operation less exposed than Oasis Hong Kong.

Taming the Market

Whether or not AirAsia X makes a success of its long-haul budget operation, history suggests that others will continue to try. Jetstar Australia has already been operating a long-haul low-fare model for some time. These operators are convinced that opportunities exist to crack open potentially large markets that are currently dissuaded from travel due to high pricing. There is no reason to believe that long-haul markets are any less price-sensitive than short-haul markets, but the recipe for success is not as simple as that of predicting the price-elasticity of demand. The challenge for long-haul low-cost operators is in controlling costs in a situation where the critical mass enjoyed by the network carriers is not available. Oasis Hong Kong was disadvantaged by a small fleet of non-standard aircraft of varying vintage. The airline was tempted to emulate the service standards of their competitors, which it was never likely to be able to match. Perhaps a more logical approach would have been to sharpen the focus by lowering product and service levels. Just as the low-cost carriers re-educated the market and altered expectations in the short-haul business, the new breed of long-haul, low-cost carriers should do the same, although service standards should obviously be better than those of one-hour flights.

Some airline chief executives are cautious about the prospects for a successful long-haul, low-cost operation. Monarch Airlines

CEO Tim Jeans says that the concept already exists. 'It's called economy class on any long-haul airline, and it's only possible because of the premium cabin on those flights.' Cathay Pacific CEO Tony Tyler points to the problem of converging operating economics between low-cost and network carriers. 'The utilisation advantage that Ryanair had over British Airways doesn't apply in long haul because we all fly our aircraft 15 hours a day. Also, the legacy carriers sell very cheap on long haul, so you've got to come in very low indeed to have much of an impact over Cathay Pacific between Europe and Asia.'

Whether we are talking about the new breed of long-haul, low-cost airline or established network carriers there is obviously an interest in improving operating efficiency and lowering costs. We have seen evidence to suggest that markets are increasingly price-sensitive and opportunities continue to abound in the emerging economies in Asia. The key to long-term success in this market segment will be in establishing a set of expectations within the market.

The low-cost phenomenon has marked a transition in the way we perceive air travel. Short-haul flights have been commodities where price is the prime determinant and not the product or service per se. In the future we will very likely see longer-haul travel begin to edge down the same path. In order for this to happen, the aircraft manufacturers have a significant role to play by producing aircraft that can be operated in a more standard fashion, and it is to this point that we now turn.

One Size Fits All

The idea of operational commonality of transport vehicles did not originate in the airline industry. The Great Western Railway in the United Kingdom was applying these principles on a mass scale nearly a century ago and, well before the jet age, had designed and built huge fleets of locomotives with standard boilers and components and standard controls, yet retaining individual performance characteristics to suit individual routes. Boeing, Airbus, Bombardier, Embraer and other smaller manufacturers have long incorporated the principles of standardisation of design and operation into their various aircraft models.

Interest in cabin design and technology has grown at an amazing rate. The first trade show to focus on the aircraft cabin, the Aircraft Interiors Expo, was held in cramped facilities in Cannes, France, in 2000. Since then the annual Expo has moved to larger facilities in Hamburg, attracting well over 10,000 visitors and is now replicated in Hong Kong and Long Beach.

The real issue is not so much the fundamental design or operation of the aircraft, but rather the seemingly endless variety of configurations available for the cabin. Flexibility of interiors is market-driven in the case of the airlines, but the manufacturers need to offer variety not only to appeal to the passenger, but also to stay one step ahead of their own competition.

However, logic suggests that it must be less expensive for airlines to fly aircraft that have broadly similar seating and equipment configurations. Operational flexibility would be enhanced, as operators could quickly and seamlessly swap aircraft between routes, and indeed, between partner airlines, with minimum disruption to spares-holding, reservation systems, and revenue management. Leasing companies could save on reconfiguration costs when aircraft are passed on to new customers. Airlines would save money on the costly customisation process. Indeed, at every stage of the production and operation cycle one can identify some degree of saving or improvement in efficiency.

So why do aircraft remain so heavily customised? It is clearly in the interests of the manufacturers to advocate standard aircraft, so long as they can continue to differentiate their aircraft models from their competitors. It is obvious that standardisation occurs in technical issues. Components, performance, maintenance, spares and many aspects of operation are clearly standardised for operational and economic reasons. However, it is very different when it comes to the aircraft cabin. Airlines still cling on to the idea that a highly differentiated airline product can command a significant premium, although the 2009 downturn revealed that the market's appetite to pay for a differentiated product has certainly diminished.

The real impetus for change must come from the airlines which need to take a fresh approach to product design and put cost reduction at the fore. Of course, nobody wants to be the first to act, for fear of ceding ground to competitors. The idea of a standard aircraft is not new, but it does seem destined to remain nirvana, despite the logic. Airlines will argue both ways, saying that they would applaud any opportunity to streamline acquisition and operating costs, but not at the expense of losing competitive advantage. Aircraft manufacturers will point to the strides they have made in improving the operational flexibility of their products but at the same time jealously guard their marketing advantages over the competition.

It would appear that the standard configured aircraft in the long-haul market is going to remain a pipe dream for a while to come. However, as air travel becomes increasingly viewed as a commodity, the time will come when investment in product competition will have to be addressed. In the 2009 crisis, premium traffic nose-dived, as the cost of air travel became less affordable in a world of greater price elasticity. Airlines that are strongly dependent on premium traffic have suddenly become vulnerable.

If any airline can solve the long-haul, low-cost puzzle and make it work, traditional long-haul operators may be forced to rethink product design. Many reputable airlines were caught napping as the short-haul, low-cost airlines took control of many markets. And, as we saw in Chapter 1, history does have a tendency to repeat itself.

Clouded Judgement

I started this chapter with an anecdote about airline service expectations and will finish with another. On 16 April 2010 I was en route from Abu Dhabi to Montreal, and became alarmed when, one hour before landing in Frankfurt, the Lufthansa captain announced that the airport would be closing after our arrival due to a cloud of volcanic ash drifting towards Germany. I will not dwell on the chaotic scenes at Frankfurt airport, replicated across Europe for days afterwards. Suffice it to say that, after three days of practically zero information about what was happening, I endured an 18-hour bus journey to Rome in order to continue my journey, finally arriving in Canada five days late.

The eruption of Eyjafjallajökull in Iceland was a Black Swan of epic proportions. It was a perfect illustration of a high-impact, hard-to-predict event that is beyond normal expectations. Although airlines reacted to the emergency in a responsible manner so far as safety is concerned, it was obvious that their customer service strategies were woefully inadequate. I believed that, as a customer of two Star Alliance member airlines, Lufthansa and Air Canada, I would be dealt with in a consistent manner. To my amazement, each airline tried to palm the responsibility for my well-being onto the other. Each had a different set of standards for hotel accommodation, and both struggled to provide timely and consistent information to stranded passengers.

I freely admit that this was an exceptional situation, and I applaud individual Lufthansa and Air Canada staff for doing their best to get me to my final destination. However, customer frustration levels were exacerbated by unnecessary confusion over details and long periods without information.

In Conclusion

The low-cost carriers deserve credit for many things. They created opportunities for more people to fly more affordably to more destinations than ever before. They spearheaded a new approach to operating efficiency. They shook the legacy carriers into reaction, with the result that they became more efficient. Indeed, in a sense, every airline has become something of a low-cost airline. Most importantly, the low-cost carriers changed the way in which passengers think about air travel, not only in the markets they serve but more generally. These changes are creating challenges for network carriers that serve a mix of long-haul and short-haul destinations, where expectations in terms of price and service clearly differ. Markets are becoming more polarised between short and long haul as a result.

Periodically, brave souls try to make a success of stand-alone long-haul, low-cost, but all attempts have so far failed. Most of the advantages that the initial wave of pure low-cost airlines devised in Europe and North America simply vanish in the long-haul arena as the economics of the two business models converge.

Short-haul air travel is slipping ever closer to being perceived as a pure commodity, although differentiation still plays an important role at the quality end of the market. However, despite a growing need for standardisation of aircraft in order to reflect the changing nature of the market as well as extract more operating efficiency, airlines still display a curious reluctance to move away from an individualistic approach to their aircraft specification. Addressing this issue, especially in short-haul markets, could be expected to yield benefits to both aircraft suppliers and operators.

In an increasingly price-conscious world, do travellers really care about brand as much as we would like to believe? I believe the answer is 'yes', but not in the sense of design and style. The focus must be on squarely on customer service, reliability and reasonable comfort, and not so much on attractive lighting effects on the aircraft ceiling. Airport designers, incidentally, fall into the same trap by designing magnificent cathedral-like buildings, with sophisticated services and opulent shopping malls. Airport forecaster Daniel Sallier believes that airports should be designed to be forgotten. 'Like the hot water supply,' he says, 'People don't think about it as long as the plumbing is working and water is pouring from the tap.'

References

BBC, 2009. 'Branson in "Patronising" Rail Ad'. 6 May. Available at: http://news.bbc.co.uk/1/hi/scotland/8035524.stm (accessed 6 May 2009).

Brandchannel, 2006. 'Asia-Pacific: A Tale of Two Sonys'. Available at: http://www.brandchannel.com/features_effect.asp?pf_id=352 (accessed 8 June 2010).

Casert, R., 2007. '13 Dots in an Airline Logo? Superstitious Complaints Prompt Change'. Available at: http://www.usatoday.com/travel/flights/2007-02-21-brussels-airlines-superstitious-fliers-logo_x.htm (accessed 6 June 2010).

Hardwick, C., 2009. 'Richard Branson Interview' (video). Available at: http://g4tv.com/attackoftheshow/exclusives/66728/richard-branson-interview.html (accessed 5 July 2009).

Interbrand, 2009. 'Best Global Brands'. Available at: http://www.interbrand.com/best_global_brands.aspx (accessed 7 June 2010).

Synovate, 2008. 'Survey Shows Ups and Downs of Air Travel'. 30 September. Available at: http://www.synovate.com/news/article/2008/09/survey-shos-ups-and-downs-of-air-travel.html (accessed 9 May 2009).

Chapter 4

'I Want To Hold Your Hand': Airline Consolidation

When we think of airline partnerships we tend to think of the three major strategic alliances – namely, Star Alliance, oneworld and SkyTeam. Between them, these three giants embrace around two-thirds of the total airline business and, although the membership structure never seems to completely settle, it is fair to say that the major alliances have achieved a position of recognition, stability and maturity. The challenges of issues such as seamless service, integrated loyalty schemes, common IT platforms and governance have been largely overcome and are certainly less controversial than they were just a few years ago.

This chapter is not about the evolution of the branded strategic alliances; it is about how airlines have worked and continue to work together in pursuit of market domination by a process of consolidation and merger. To do this we must delve into a murky world of self-interest and consumer choice. We must look at how the most fiercely competitive market of all, the North Atlantic, has become controlled by a handful of strong players. We will see how many big name airlines have shamelessly colluded in order to eliminate competition. Like many themes of this book, there are distinct ways of looking at the matter: an airline business perspective and a passenger perspective, where objectives and motives are frequently on a collision course.

The Urge to Merge

In the bad old days, before open-skies treaties reinvigorated the airline industry and championed the consumer, and before phrases such as 'anti-trust immunity' troubled the airline lexicon, airline chiefs devised a cosy and gentlemanly way of protecting their businesses. Cut-throat competition in the open market was much too unseemly for the early generation of manager. Why not sit in a room, under the aegis of IATA, and thrash out what fares to charge and what services to offer? Naturally, such an archaic system offered no incentive to work towards efficiency. A regulated price structure was an effective way of immunising the airlines from dangerous competition. Furthermore, governments in the pre-deregulation world held enormous sway in this protectionist strategy, being heavily influenced by matters of sovereignty and national pride.

When the open-skies world came along, governments had to subvert their desire to protect individual companies in order to refocus on the rights of consumers and the efficiency of the industry as a whole. After the United States led the way with domestic deregulation in 1978, the European Union adopted an equally encouraging liberal attitude. However, it can be argued that those halcyon days are well and truly over. Governments have become cannier, more receptive to whispers from corporate lobbyists and more concerned about risks to their national champions posed by new breeds of upstart airline, especially the low-cost carriers. To be blunt, the major airlines wanted governments to acquiesce to as much consolidation as could be handled, backed up with anti-trust immunity. Major carriers craved as much protection as they could muster, and they largely got it.

It is worth pointing out that there are some quite legitimate reasons for airlines to merge. It makes perfect sense to consolidate airlines that have small overlapping hubs into a single airline with a stronger hub. The merger of Northwest Airlines and Republic in the United States, or that of Air France with Air Inter, fall into this category. Another legitimate reason would be to fold a bankrupt, or potentially bankrupt, airline into a stronger airline with a view to creating a more viable and streamlined operation, and critically take unsustainable capacity out of the market at the same time. The Lufthansa merger with SWISS would be a good example of this approach.

Around the turn of the century commentators began arguing that the airline industry is ripe for more consolidation. This 'urge to merge' did not come from the marketplace, but from the large airlines themselves. The benefits are always offered up in the same way: opportunities for rationalisation that can only come through single organisations, the benefits of broader networks and associated synergies, easier access to capital and so on.

Hubert Horan is a US-based consultant with interesting credentials, having overseen the development of the original KLM–Northwest alliance network in 1992. Horan points to four principal objections to current consolidation activity. First, recent mergers have involved intercontinental carriers in markets that are typically robust, profitable and stable. This goes against the idea that consolidation should be designed to shore up failing operations. Second, there is little evidence to suggest that consolidation is actually removing excess capacity from the market. So, by reducing the number of competitors in the market and maintaining capacity levels, we are getting the worst of both worlds. Third, the capital markets have been reluctant to step in and invest in airline mergers, leaving consolidating airlines to indulge in stock swaps. Fourth, major intercontinental markets, such as the North Atlantic, have significant barriers to entry, not in the sense of obtaining traffic rights but in the sense of acquiring slots at congested airports and simply gearing up in order to run a complex operation with expensive capacity. Although the North Atlantic market is inherently liberal, it has frequently proven to be a crushingly disappointing market for many would-be Davids facing the industry's Goliaths. Says Horan, 'What we've ended up with in the last five years is basically the complete elimination of competition on the North Atlantic. Twenty-six independent competitors have been merged into three. You've got a cartel of three collusive alliances with the two groups led by Lufthansa and Air France having a stranglehold on all markets from the US to continental Europe and the American Airlines and British Airways partnership set to dominate the UK market.'

There is nothing inherently wrong with mergers or anti-trust immunity. What Hubert Horan is challenging is the use of these instruments to bring about extraordinary reductions in competition. In 2003 the top two and top three carriers on North Atlantic routes between the United States and continental Europe boasted 41 per cent and 65 per cent of the market respectively. Just five years later the three alliance groups, which formerly comprised 26 independent competitors, controlled a staggering 98 per cent of that market (see Figure 4.1). Says Horan, 'This had nothing to do with market forces, where efficient carriers drive out inefficient carriers. This was the big airlines running to governments, sitting in a back room and asking permission to artificially eliminate competition.' Strong stuff.

Departure share of US to Continental Europe market

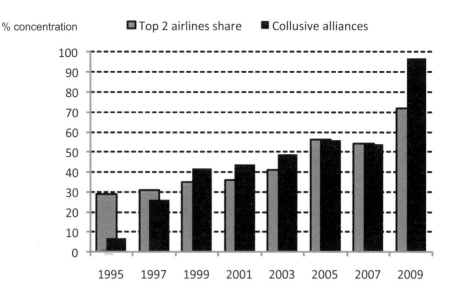

Figure 4.1   North Atlantic concentration
Source: DOT Form 41.

Yet Patrick Bianquis, Vice President Alliances of Air France–KLM and the architect of the operational hub of Charles de Gaulle airport in Paris, disagrees, arguing that consolidation is a natural trend in an industry that is less consolidated than many others. 'We are still a very fragmented industry,' he says, 'and the North Atlantic is nowhere near a monopoly.' Bianquis makes the point that the EU–US open-skies agreement did not yield expected benefits. 'Even though SkyTeam was quite strong on the North Atlantic, the London to Los Angeles route was not a success, and if Air France had been alone it would have been even worse.' Bianquis believes that home markets will still be flown by the major carrier of every country, but competition will exist between the various groupings. Thus, Lufthansa and United work together to serve the Germany to US market, competing with Delta and Air France–KLM. 'If we were not with Delta maybe they would have difficulty sustaining their flights,' he says.

Critics argue that there are substantial risks associated with consolidation and that true economies of scale have proven elusive in the past. Labour contracts can prove an especially difficult hurdle. For example, the US Airways and America West merger in 2005 was largely contingent upon maintaining separate, rather than integrating, pilot contracts.

The biggest concern raised by critics of collusive partnerships centres on the risk of pricing abuse. However, it can be shown that such behaviour is not at all confined to the alliances or consolidated structures.

Succumbing to Temptation

Coordinating pricing under the protection of anti-trust immunity is not the same thing as surreptitious meetings between airlines with no protection from the competition laws in order to fix prices and gouge consumers. Astonishingly, some of the biggest names in the airline business have had their names sullied by criminal accusations over the last few years and the regulators are getting tougher. There have been two high-profile cases so far. British Airways and Virgin Atlantic, long thought to be constantly at each other's throats, were accused of secretly conspiring to fix fuel surcharges on long-haul flights between 2004 and 2006. Both airlines have been publicly contrite, apologising for the actions of a small number of senior members of staff, but their shiny images were nevertheless tarnished. British Airways was reportedly fined around £270 million by the UK and US authorities, although, perhaps in an act of rough justice, Virgin Atlantic escaped a fine as they had blown the whistle in the first place (Kollewe 2009).

The second high-profile case concerns investigations by the UK, US, Canadian and Australian competition authorities, as well as the FBI, into cargo rate fixing between 2001 and 2006. The allegations are centred on a global conspiracy to fleece customers by driving up shipping rates, fuel surcharges and security costs. Incredibly, at least 15 airlines in Europe, the Gulf, Asia and

Australia have been investigated, raided or otherwise accused of the dastardly deeds. The US Department of Justice announced criminal fines totalling an astonishing US$504 million to be paid by those airlines pleading guilty, namely Air France–KLM, Cathay Pacific, Martinair Holland and SAS Cargo Group. Previous fines had been levied on British Airways, Qantas Airways, Korean Air and Japan Airlines. Associate Attorney General Kevin O'Connor has referred to the activities as an 'international price-fixing cartel', claiming that the fines represented one of the largest criminal fines ever imposed by the Department of Justice (DoJ 2008).

Clearly, left to their own devices, the airlines are not always to be trusted. The cargo cartel scandal is evidence enough that the European Commission and the US Department of Transportation have their work cut out to keep the biggest names in the business in check. After all, the ultimate objective is to make sure that the consumer is not being fleeced. Yet over the last few years we have seen the emergence of collaborations that are quasi-collusive in nature and raise questions about anti-competitive and oligopolistic behaviour. This trend suggests a transition from a phase in which markets have been dominated by the three major alliance groupings to a new phase in which consolidation is effectively handing the keys to a small group of mega-carriers that command huge potential influence. Let's see how the industry has managed to get to this situation.

The Success of Alliances

A typical strategic alliance may be described as a formal association between two or more parties, with an aim to advance mutually beneficial and common interests. To make such a partnership work, five principal conditions should be in place. First, the alliance should have an identifiable organisational structure with clear governance. Second, there should be evident and equal benefits to all parties. Third, there must be alignment of overall business objectives, including common vision, targets and planning processes, including fleet replacement strategies. Fourth, the product itself should be aligned, which means coordinated operations, branding, aircraft interior configurations, joint loyalty schemes and so on. Fifth, the supply chain and infrastructure should be integrated, with common service and maintenance providers, IT platform and applications, and joint purchasing contracts.

All three strategic alliance groupings have achieved considerable success in these five principal conditions. All will point to an improvement in traffic feed, access to previously restricted markets, development of ever-intricate itineraries and travel opportunities through hubs and, of course, cost savings. All will claim a significant bottom-line revenue improvement, in terms of both growth revenue and incremental margin, and this is usually measured in hundreds of millions of dollars. For example, when oneworld celebrated its tenth anniversary in 2009 it boasted a total of revenue of US$5 billion from alliance fares and joint sales over the life of the alliance. Furthermore, two-thirds of this amount, an amazing US$3 billion, was claimed as 'incremental revenue' or revenue that would not have accrued if the alliance had never existed (Dunn 2009). It is worth pointing out the rather obvious fact that people do not travel more just because their chosen airline happens to be part of a strategic alliance. So, if the alliance members' revenues are *all* increasing, does this not suggest that somebody else's revenue has been plundered?

Leaving the strategic alliances aside for a moment, it is worth considering an example of how a unified approach to airline operation can yield benefit. A fine example can be found in Latin America, where the LAN group of airlines cooperates closely to deploy its common fleet of 767 aircraft in different countries. LAN's Planning Schedule Director Patricio Jaramillo explains, 'We have 27 767-300s and each has the same configuration; that is the key to fly the aircraft in LAN Chile, LAN Peru and LAN Ecuador. The integrated approach to the assignment of aircraft across different countries facilitates growth in a manner that benefits all airlines in the grouping.' There is a single back-up aircraft for the integrated operation, based in Santiago (see Figures 4.2 and 4.3). The value of the combined operation even extends to the crews – for example, some Chilean crews fly in Peru, although the authorities do encourage LAN to take crews from individual countries in the partnership. What this illustrates is that an airline does not necessarily need to be in a strategic alliance in order to

767-300 rotation

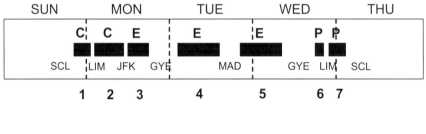

SCL   Santiago de Chile   **C** LAN Chile
LIM   Lima   **E** LAN Ecuador
JFK   New York   **P** LAN Peru
MAD   Madrid
GYE   Guayaquil

Times are corrected to SCL local time
Block hours: 46.75

Figure 4.2   LAN airlines cooperative fleet-sharing – 1
Source: LAN airlines, personal communication.

767-300 rotation

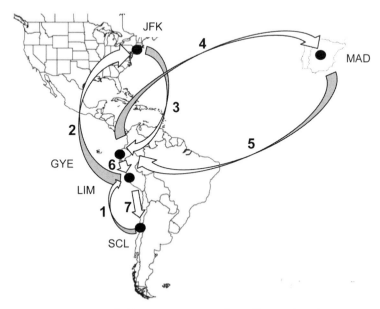

Figure 4.3   LAN airlines cooperative fleet-sharing – 2
Source: LAN airlines, personal communication.

extract operating synergies and cost reduction. As long as airlines can harmonise their product strategies, aircraft configurations and operating schedules, then economies of operation are easily achievable.

Consolidation has taken root within Latin America, incidentally. Avianca has formed a joint venture with Grupo TACA in a quest to generate new revenues and reduce costs. The potential for this merger looks promising as the overlap between the existing operations was minimal. More consolidation in the region could be on the way.

A slightly unusual alliance was formed in 2009 between two low-cost carriers. Jetstar, the low-cost operation of Qantas, formed a strategic alliance with Malaysia's AirAsia. The scope of the alliance is limited to engineering cooperation, joint handling and helping each other's passengers in the event of disrupted services. One particularly interesting development is that the parties are prepared to cooperate on aircraft specifications and procurement. Excluded from the arrangement are code shares and equity exchange. This alliance may certainly be termed 'strategic' but not at all in the sense of the three major global groupings of Star, oneworld and SkyTeam.

Smaller airlines may even shun the idea of joining a strategic alliance. Sri Lankan Airlines, for example, had a partnership with Emirates for many years, which included participation in a common frequent-flyer programme. Sri Lankan's head of commercial planning, Manique Gunasekera, says, 'I think one may lose one's identity in an alliance. Although it is not something that we are saying "no" to, we are not actively pursuing the idea.'

Larger airlines take a different view. For them, being in an alliance is all about power and control.

Mega Mania Takes Hold

The emergence of new consolidated airline structures has crept upon us, almost by stealth, and has led to a renewal of fears that consumer choices are becoming more limited. The first move was made in late 2003 when Air France and KLM Royal Dutch Airlines announced their intention to merge using an innovative joint venture structure. Approvals from the European Commission and US Department of Justice were quickly followed by the creation of a unique (certainly for the airline business) form of organisational structure whereby both airlines would retain their individual brands, and the shares of a merged entity, called Air France–KLM, would be traded on stock exchanges. The new holding company was set up with 81 per cent ownership by private shareholders (including former Air France and KLM shareholders) and the remainder held by the French government. Both airlines would operate with a common bottom line. For KLM, it was their third time at the altar, following a collapsed agreement with Alitalia and a proposed merger with British Airways. The tie-up was not without significant risk. For example, cultural differences between the Dutch and the French were an acknowledged challenge. French corporate culture is notoriously hierarchical, unlike in the Netherlands, and, as anyone who has ever negotiated with the Dutch will know, you need to have a thick skin. However, everyone was conscious of the risks and they were overcome. Importantly, the existing Air France and KLM networks had little overlap, so it was a relatively easy matter to grow the market of the combined airline. The two principal hubs of Amsterdam and Paris are only 400 kilometres apart and would henceforth cooperate as a dual hub operation rather than compete with each other. In terms of numbers of passengers, Paris Charles de Gaulle and Amsterdam airports are ranked third and fourth respectively, and each has development potential. The combined operation could, even at its inception, connect with over 100 long-haul destinations, exceeding the offers of either British Airways or Lufthansa. To cap it all, the value delivered by the combined Air France–KLM operation actually exceeded projections, with the majority of benefits coming from coordination of sales activities, plus some optimisation of the network and schedules.

Air France has calculated that the benefit of the merger amounted to €790 million from 2004 to 2009 (Air France–KLM 2009). From the airlines' perspective, the entire exercise has been a glowing success. Air France–KLM turned a net profit of €748 million in the year ending 31 March 2008, against operating revenues of €24,114 billion (Katyan's Lounge 2009), although the operating margin of 3 per cent (ratio of revenues and profits) was at best typical for the industry, but paltry compared to other industrial sectors. Air France already owns 25 per cent of that perennial problem child of Europe, Alitalia, and will doubtless increase its stake over time.

Acquisition Fever Accelerates

It was not long before Lufthansa stirred. In the summer of 2007 the German carrier successfully and professionally executed the acquisition of Swiss International Airlines. Although the detail differs, the element that had been so crucial in the Air France–KLM link-up, namely keeping individual identity of the two brands, was retained. Born out of the ashes of the failed Swissair in 2002, Swiss International Airlines had been struggling with a worsening financial situation, exacerbated by rising competition from low-cost carriers. So, an offer of €310 million from Lufthansa was not to be sniffed at. Approvals from the US and European regulators were swiftly obtained, although the EU competition commissioner insisted that the combined operation should relinquish slots at the Zurich and Frankfurt hubs, as well as Munich, Düsseldorf, Berlin, Vienna, Stockholm and Copenhagen. The effect was to gift up to 41 round trips to potential competitors. Lufthansa was certainly not troubled by the concession and trumpeted early profits. The acquisition of SWISS by Lufthansa also occasioned the movement of SWISS from the oneworld into the Star Alliance.

Lufthansa announced in their 2007 annual report that sustainable synergies arising from the integration of SWISS amounted to €233 million, being 'considerably above' projections. Importantly for the SWISS people, who had suffered the ignominy of the demise of their prized Swissair just a few years earlier, this acquisition of their national airline was seen in a positive light. Key to the success was respect for SWISS identity.

But Lufthansa was not finished yet. British carrier bmi, formerly British Midland, had for years been a Cinderella of the Star Alliance owing to its command of around 11 per cent of the slots at London's Heathrow. Lufthansa already owned 30 per cent of the carrier and decided in 2008 to acquire the stake of majority owner Sir Michael Bishop. Having won regulatory approval for the deal from the UK Department of Transport, the Civil Aviation Authority and the European Commission, the £350 million sale looked assured. But bmi's 2008 losses of close to £100 million clearly gave Lufthansa cold feet and it tried to wriggle out of the deal. Undismayed, Bishop resorted to the High Court to enforce the sale, and Lufthansa grudgingly settled the deal out of court (Robertson 2009). Since the sale was concluded Lufthansa has curiously held talks with other suitors for bmi, reported to include British Airways and Virgin Atlantic Airways. One can understand Virgin's interest, as a combined bmi–Virgin operation would make life ever-so-slightly more uncomfortable for British Airways at Heathrow. In any case, Lufthansa could never realistically capture access to sufficient Heathrow slots to worry British Airways. It remains to be seen whether Cinderella-like bmi can live happily ever after.

Lufthansa's appetite for acquisitions seems undiminished. The European Commission granted approval for it to take over Brussels Airlines, which subsequently joined the Star Alliance, and, with the takeover of Austrian Airlines in 2009, Lufthansa overtook Air France–KLM as Europe's largest carrier. Lufthansa makes no apology for its vigorous shopping spree, believing that the enlarged entity is good for customers as well as shareholders. Indeed, CEO Wolfgang Mayrhuber said that critical mass is essential to survive cutthroat competition and this can only be achieved through alliances, competitive position or mergers (Jeske 2007).

The Mother of All Mergers

While executives in Air France and Lufthansa were quietly marshalling their empires in Europe, a rather similar pattern was emerging in the United States. The acquisition of US Airways by America West in 2005 was the first significant US airline merger for a number of years. These were two struggling airlines operating in different markets, deploying different strategies and with different cultures. The idea was to create a sort of major low-cost carrier from two struggling entities. However, designation of the letters 'LCC' as the airline stock symbol was never going to be enough. The inside joke at the time was that this strategy should have been called, 'Extreme Makeover – Airline Edition'. Despite these criticisms, the merged entity did turn in a profit of $303 million in its first full year of operation. CEO Doug Parker understood that US Airways would never really be on the world stage unless it pursued further consolidation, although a subsequent bid for bankrupt Delta Air Lines got nowhere.

The US Airways and America West link-up turned out to be the first in a new wave of merger mania. Continental and United conducted some discussions in 2008, but they stalled. However, when Continental abandoned SkyTeam in favour of the Star Alliance in 2009 the merger possibility was suddenly back on the table. However, just as with US Airways and America West, the primary motive to merge appeared to be driven mostly by dire financial considerations, rather than a coherent strategic plan.

The biggest of them all, however, was the merger of Delta and Northwest, announced in April 2008. As in the case of the two mega-mergers in Europe both the protagonists were serving complementary, rather than competing, markets. Delta had been historically dominant in the south-east and Northwest Airlines in the northern part of the United States. Critically, Northwest was operating a series of routes across the Pacific to Asia and Delta was serving Europe. Press releases trumpeted the benefits of global connectivity and the fact that none of the existing hubs would be eliminated, although nothing was said about the number of flights. The biggest eye-opener was that the annual revenue and cost synergies were predicted as more than US$1 billion, coming from more effective aircraft utilisation, an enhanced route network and reduced overhead and improved operational efficiency. Let's consider the scale of this operation. The combined airline, which retained the Delta name, served 390 destinations in 67 countries, generating annual revenues of around US$35 billion, operating a mainline fleet of about 750 mainline aircraft and employing 75,000 people worldwide. By some margin, this is a monumental operation. In fact, as individual entities, both Delta and Northwest were relatively prosperous in the middle of 2008, compared with other US major carriers. Second-quarter operating profits were US$248 million for Delta and US$162 million for Northwest, and, despite higher fuel prices in the third quarter, Delta's profits only slipped to US$125 million whilst Northwest sustained a loss of

US$170 million. Even though the two airlines were outperforming other major carriers in the United States, the figures were dismal compared to the same period in 2007, when the third-quarter operating profits were US$422 million and US$460 million respectively. By the end of 2008 the situation had become critical, with Delta losing US$56 million in the last quarter and Northwest losing US$441 million (Bureau of Transportation 2008).

At the time of the merger the Delta and Northwest fleets were almost entirely dissimilar. Delta's 441 active aircraft (as at November 2009) comprised predominantly Boeing models, eight different types (see Figure 4.4) and four separate technology platforms (737, 757/767, 777 and MD). Northwest's fleet of 304 active aircraft comprised a mixture of Boeing and Airbus models, nine different types (see Figure 4.4) and five separate technologies (Airbus, 747 Classic, 747-400, 757 and DC9). Out of the grand total of 745 aircraft, only 163 757-200s were common to both fleets. The combined number of ordered and optioned aircraft in November 2009 was 162, but among them there was not a single overlap between the existing fleets. Clearly, bolting together such a huge fleet of 16 different types, many with different crew and

Operational fleets as at 22 November 2009

Delta Air Lines				Northwest Airlines
Unique to Delta Air Lines				Unique to Northwest Airlines
737-700, -800	**81**	**126**	A319, A320
767-300, -400	**92**	**30**	A330-200, -300
777-200	**16**	**6**	747-200
MD88, 90	**130**	**16**	747-400
		16	757-300
		69	DC9-30

Common
122   **41**
757-200

Total	**441**	**304**

Figure 4.4   Delta and Northwest Airlines fleet composition

Source: Author's data.

maintenance requirements, is not easy, and scale economies are unlikely at this level.

Elephants in the Room?

British Airways has long hankered to extend its influence, and the development of the two major European groupings led by Air France–KLM and Lufthansa surely acted as a catalyst to accelerate this ambition. It was not a huge surprise when, in November 2009, British Airways and Iberia signed a memorandum of understanding that will lead to a merged operation. There was talk of redundancies, and CEO Willie Walsh forecast synergies of €400 million after five years, most of it coming from combined fleets, maintenance operations and various back-office functions. Also unsurprisingly, British Airways' competitors were less than impressed. Virgin Atlantic's CEO, Steve Ridgeway, spoke of a 'monster monopoly' and Ryanair's O'Leary likened the merger to 'two drunks leaning on each other', arguing that if you combine one high-fare, loss-making airline with another, you end up with another airline charging high fares and making even more losses (Rothwell 2009).

In fact, loss-making airlines have taken on an uncanny appeal for the burgeoning giants to gobble up. Japan Air Lines, a oneworld member and already the recipient of no less than three government bail-outs since 2001, was in a parlous state by the end of 2009, weighed down by US$11 billion of debt. Bankruptcy seemed a logical outcome, but JAL suddenly found itself courted by the giants, who brushed aside the negatives and swooped in with juicy funding offers. First, a Delta-led initiative on behalf of SkyTeam announced a package in excess of $1 billion, comprising an equity injection, revenue guarantees, asset-backed funding and even a transition package to cover the cost of leaving oneworld and moving to SkyTeam. American Airlines quickly countered with what must be presumed to be a superior offer, and eventually JAL was persuaded to stay with oneworld. Obviously, rescue packages of such magnitude could only be funded by either government or equity investors, rather than the airlines themselves. How ironic that the scrap over JAL, an airline with plainly gigantic problems, should be conducted by airlines themselves struggling to keep their heads above water.

The JAL case is a perfect illustration of a favourite airline industry tradition of sparing failing carriers from their ultimate doom. I asked consolidation expert Hubert Horan for his opinion on the Japan–US open-skies treaty of 2009. 'It will have a huge practical effect,' he shot back. 'It will massively reduce competition and massively increase fares. If JAL was in any other country it would have been liquidated 15 years ago. Will protecting JAL allow US carriers to flood the market with lower fares? I don't think so. It's Orwellian to agree massive subsidies for inefficient carriers with huge restrictions on who can serve which airport in an open-skies treaty'. Horan's point is that the Japanese market is incontestable due to chronic congestion. 'What you're seeing is a counter revolution against the whole deregulation movement,' he argues.

In Conclusion

Mergers in the United States are being driven by very different factors than in Europe. Most of the US major airlines have been in and out of bankruptcy, some of them more than once. Virtually all have suffered serious losses due to the economic downturn, and most are struggling to access capital and financing to replace increasingly elderly fleets, which make them particularly vulnerable to high fuel prices. In short, they are well and truly trapped. The main problem in the United States is that the traditional airlines are forced to concentrate on the domestic market and defend their hubs and, in addition, need to face up to competition from the new breed of lower-cost carrier. They are intent on raw survival, whereas the European carriers are intent on dominating international routes and markets. However, that strategy depends on chipping into every single market, marginalising competition and bolstering pricing. It is hard to see how else they can do it. Frankly, these mega airlines were already big enough to extract maximum economies of scale *before* they merged, so their only hope is revenue, and the only way to boost revenue is to create a stranglehold on the market.

It is too difficult and too early to say whether the naysayers are right and that customers will be materially disadvantaged by a perceived reduction in competitive choice. However, in exchange for regulatory approval and anti-trust immunity, the merging airlines have been obliged to make some concessions by surrendering slots, although such conditions have never been particularly severe.

Supporters of the mega-mergers argue that they are essential in order to propagate the economies of scale and market reach necessary to weather downturns. Yet gigantic mergers do not burst into existence at the flick of a switch. Apart from the time needed to plan a potential partnership and time needed to obtain clearance from competition authorities, there is obviously an extended period necessary to bring about myriad practical elements. These could typically include resolving pilot contracts and seniority issues, integrating different workforces and cultures, combining route networks, integrating reservation and revenue management systems, streamlining the supply chain, rationalising fleet composition and harmonising the order book. It is blindingly obvious that sorting out these issues is likely to take an extended period of time and incur a cost.

The potential impact of the new mega-mergers is greater than that of any of the major branded alliances, which Horan sees as ending up as little more than vehicles for enhanced loyalty programmes, code-sharing and joint lounges. Certainly, when looking at the recent history of the mega-mergers it is doubtful whether the traditional prerequisites of a cost-effective marriage, such as fleet synergies, for example, played a significant role. Rather, the urge to merge has been driven by something far more elemental: market domination, no matter what. And the rest of us had better get used to the idea.

References

Air France–KLM, 2009. 'Accelerating Initiatives to Increase Synergies'. Available at: http://www.airfranceklm-finance.com/air-france-klm-strategy.html (accessed 15 December 2009).
Bureau of Transportation Statistics, 2008. 'Second Quarter 2008 System Airline Financial Data: Network Airlines Report Growing Loss Margin'.

Available at: http://www.bts.gov/press_releases/2008/bts045_08/html/bts045_08.html (accessed 15 December 2009).

Department of Justice, 2008. 'Major International Airlines Agree to Plead Guilty and Pay Criminal Fines Totaling More than $500 Million for Fixing Prices on Air Cargo Rates'. 26 June. Available at: http://www.justice.gov/atr/public/press_releases/2008/234435.htm (accessed 20 November 2009).

Dunn, G., 2009. 'Oneworld Touts $5b Revenues from Alliance over First 10 Years'. 3 February. Available at: http://www.flightglobal.com/articles/2009/02/03/322031/oneworld-touts-5b-revenues-from-alliance-over-first-10.html (accessed 10 December 2009).

Jeske, J., 2007. 'We Have to Grow – We Will Grow'. March. Available at: http://www.atlantic-times.com/archive_detail.php?recordID=813 (accessed 20 December 2009).

Katyan's Lounge, 2009. 'Air France–KLM Merger, In Retrospect'. 14 November. Available at: http://loungereview.wordpress.com/2009/11/14/air-france-klm-merger-in-retrospect-/ (accessed 9 June 2010).

Kollewe, J., 2009. 'Virgin Atlantic Chief Comes Clean over Knowledge of Airline Price-fixing with British Airways'. 14 July. Available at: http://www.guardian.co.uk/business/2009/jul/14/british-airways-virgin-atlantic-cartel-case (accessed 14 July 2009).

Robertson, D., 2009. 'Sir Michael Bishop in Court Bid to Force Lufthansa Merger'. *The Times*, 21 May 2009.

Rothwell, S., 2009. 'British Airways, Iberia Agree to $7 Billion Merger (Update 3)'. 13 November. Available at: http://www.bloomberg.com/apps/news?pid=newsarchive&sid=aJn_DQvhFM24 (accessed 2 December 2009).

Chapter 5

'You Never Give Me Your Money': Pricing and Revenue Management

Consider this exchange between a shopkeeper in a hardware store and a customer:

> Customer: Hi, how much is your paint?
>
> Shopkeeper: We have regular quality for 12 dollars a gallon and premium for 18 dollars. How many gallons would you like?
>
> Customer: Five gallons of regular quality, please.
>
> Shopkeeper: Great. That will be 60 dollars plus tax.

There seems nothing unusual about that exchange. Now let's imagine that the customer is buying the paint not from a hardware store, but from an airline:

> Customer: Hi, how much is your paint?
>
> Clerk: Well, sir, that all depends.
>
> Customer: Depends on what?
>
> Clerk: Well, actually a lot of things.
>
> Customer: How about just giving me an average price?
>
> Clerk: Wow, that's a hard question. The lowest price is nine dollars a gallon, and we have 150 prices up to about 200 dollars a gallon.
>
> Customer: What's the difference in the paint?
>
> Clerk: Oh, there isn't any difference; it's all the same paint.
>
> Customer: Well then, I'd like some nine-dollar paint.

Clerk: Well, first I need to ask you a few questions. When do you intend to use it?

Customer: I want to paint tomorrow, on my day off.

Clerk: Sir, the paint for tomorrow is the 200-dollar paint.

Customer: What? When would I have to paint in order to get the nine-dollar version?

Clerk: That would be in three weeks, but you will also have to agree to start painting before Friday of that week and continue painting until at least Sunday.

Customer: You've got to be kidding!

Clerk: Sir, we don't kid around here. Of course, I'll have to check to see if we have any of that paint available before I can sell it to you.

Customer: What do you mean, 'check to see if you can sell it to me'? You have shelves full of the stuff; I can see it right there.

Clerk: Just because you can see it doesn't mean that we have it. It may be the same paint, but we only sell a certain number of gallons on any given weekend. Oh, and by the way, the price just went to 12 dollars.

Customer: What! You mean the price just went up while we were talking!

Clerk: Yes, sir. You see, we change prices and rules thousands of times a day, and since you haven't actually walked out of the store with your paint yet, we just decided to change. Unless you want the same thing to happen again, I would suggest that you get on with your purchase. How many gallons do you want?

Customer: I don't know exactly. Maybe five gallons. Maybe I should buy six gallons just to make sure I have enough.

Clerk: Oh no, sir, you can't do that. If you buy the paint and then don't use it you will be liable for penalties and possible confiscation of the paint you already have.

Customer: What?

Clerk: That's right. We can sell you enough paint to do your kitchen, bathroom, hall and north bedroom, but if you stop painting before you do the bedroom, you will be in violation of our tariffs.

Customer: But what does it matter to you whether I use all the paint? I already paid you for it!

Clerk: Sir, there's no point in getting upset; that's just the way it is. We make plans based on the idea that you will use all the paint and, when you don't, it just causes all sorts of problems.

Customer: This is crazy! I suppose something terrible will happen if I don't keep painting until after Saturday night?

Clerk: Yes, sir, it will.

Customer: Well, that does it! I'm going somewhere else to buy my paint.

Clerk: That won't do you any good, sir. We all have the same rules. Oh, and thanks for flying – I mean painting – with our airline. (Hess 1998)

In fact, the exchange is not so crazy. This brilliantly Pythonesque sketch, which first appeared in 1998, reveals the sinister side of how airlines manipulate pricing in order to eke the highest overall revenue from their customers. Of course, it seems impertinent and objectionable that the hardware-store clerk should goad his customer into revealing personal details about how he intends to use his paint. Yet this, and every other element in that discussion, is no different to what happens when we buy an airline ticket.

Scam or Saviour?

I happily acknowledge that revenue management, far from being the nemesis of the bargain-hunter, has been a highly successful and vital strategic tool in numerous industries. Hotels, restaurants, conference and function providers, car-hire companies, advertisers, karaoke bars and golf courses have all been beneficiaries of the work of a dedicated band of researchers and mathematicians who created the algorithms that form the core of revenue management systems.

The airline industry was one of the first to realise that the cocktail of inflexible capacity, variable demand, segmentable markets, and control over pricing and inventory could be considered as a single problem to be measured, predicted and finally optimised. It was the US majors, such as American Airlines, and their former chief executive Bob Crandall, in particular, who championed the original development of what was then called yield management. But managing yields is only one component of the puzzle. Balancing all the ingredients of the cocktail so that overall revenues are improved is a task of such sophistication and complexity that revenue management has become essential.

A powerful revenue management system can improve revenues by several percentage points, even if all players in a market apply the techniques. In this respect, revenue management is not a zero-sum game like, for example, frequent-flyer or loyalty programmes. Practically every airline in a competitive market operates some form of loyalty scheme as they understand that many travel decisions are motivated by juicy offers of reward miles and points. The promise of reward certainly attracts the market, and this has been beneficial to airlines. However, when every airline is doing the same thing, the advantages are temporary, and the positive effect eventually cancels out when every player in the market adopts the same approach. Ironically, once every airline has a loyalty programme, every airline must bear the cost of administration as well as assume the liability of capacity reserved to liquidate members' mileage accounts.

Unsurprisingly, frequent-flyer and loyalty programmes are extremely popular. Loyal customers have that cosy feeling that airlines dote on them, with enticing gifts. Psychology plays a role here. The offer of reward creates an erroneous feeling of getting something for nothing, even though most people will cheerfully admit that nothing is ever free. The point is that loyalty programmes do not carry any undertones of trickery, whereas travellers do harbour suspicion about airline pricing tactics.

Let me say again that the designers, providers and operators of revenue management tools are honest and reputable people who have delivered value to airlines and their customers. I know for a fact that there is a genuine belief in the community that their forecasting techniques are scientifically proven and objective. So, before looking at the 'dark side', I must address the ways in which revenue management benefits the consumer.

Louis Busuttil is an industry expert in the subject of revenue management, with a lifetime's experience of implementing systems in major airlines and conducting operational audits to identify how revenue management can help improve financial results. He cites a number of reasons why consumers are better off, and these are worth exploring.

First, although it is clearly true that the Internet has gifted consumers with more command over their purchasing decisions, it is also the case that the seller has also benefited from increased power. This is because the Internet allows a degree of fine-tuning of price that was simply unavailable in earlier times. Thus, it is easily possible to make very small adjustments to price in response to equally small fluctuations in demand. Moreover, these changes can be made rapidly and cost-effectively. Therefore, to revert to the paint analogy, the non-revenue managed situation (where the customer was asked to pay a multiple of the regular unit price) is akin to a blunderbuss approach to pricing. There is no finesse at all. However, revenue management techniques allow a forensic approach to pricing, which should mean that the consumer is being asked to pay according to precisely calculated principles and conditions. This leads directly to the delicate balance of motivation between seller and buyer.

There is no question that buyers have considerable power, as they can shop around and compare offers rapidly and easily. The real issue is whether travellers are flexible and organised. Flexible travellers have total liberty to alter their schedules to gain access to lower prices (that were notably absent in the non-revenue managed paint shop exchange.) Organised travellers have the opportunity to plan their travel in advance and can be rewarded by being granted access to lower fares. Late bookers, such as price-inelastic business travellers, must pay for the privilege of expecting capacity to be available to them at short notice. So, the critical factor is the number of days prior to travel that a booking is made. A well-managed seller should have an advantage over a disorganised buyer who makes a travel decision very close to day of departure. To quote Louis Busuttil, 'Happily for the sellers, there are a lot of disorganised, last-minute buyers in the world'.

Busuttil points to other key reasons why revenue management directly benefits the consumer. An effective overbooking strategy should raise average load factors, which improves the economic efficiency of the aircraft, and which in turn *can* be passed on to the end consumer in the form of cheaper fares. Whether fares are actually lowered as a direct consequence of a successful overbooking strategy is, in my view, a moot point. Certainly, the opportunity to reduce fares without compromising profits exists, but an airline is obviously more likely to exercise this option for competitive, rather than altruistic, reasons.

Airlines can ensure that there are always enough seats available on any flight at the time of departure (albeit at a high price) through pricing discrimination and demand manipulation. Therefore, the argument goes, the consumer benefits since very urgent travel can always be accommodated.

Dr Peter Belobaba, Principal Research Scientist at the Department of Aeronautics and Astronautics, Massachusetts Institute of Technology, is one of the progenitors of revenue management. He is adamant that, without revenue management, airlines would be charging a single price on each of their routes that would be substantially higher than today's low average price, and passengers would be flying in smaller aircraft with less frequency. He says, 'It is easily shown that systematic forecasting and optimisation protects seats for high-paying passengers, but makes an enormous number of seats available to low-fare passengers.' Belobaba is convinced that airlines would be unable to cover their costs if they did not practise differential pricing and revenue management.

Another leading proponent of revenue management is Sabre Airline Solutions, which markets its own revenue management software, AirMax, as well as acting as a global distribution system. Jim Barlow, Senior Vice President Passenger Solutions, endorses both Louis Busuttil's and Peter Belobaba's views, adding, 'An airline that did not practise revenue management would provide less service, maybe fewer flight attendants, less amenities, or reduce their schedule so you would not have the flexibility.'

We can safely conclude, then, that revenue management is good for us.

And Now, the Dark Side

Picture the scene: a departure gate at Stockholm's Arlanda airport, on a busy weekday early afternoon. A full complement of mostly business passengers waits patiently to be called to board a flight to London. A calm announcement asks if any passengers might be willing to fly on a later flight. Practically everyone in a suit stops working on their laptop, or discards their newspaper. Ears are pricked, eyes directed at the SAS Scandinavian Airlines agent with the microphone. But nobody moves. A few minutes later, the agent makes another announcement. This time there is money on the table. Five checked-in passengers are being offered a financial inducement to take the later flight. Now, the suited brigade start looking at each other, but still nobody makes a move. Minutes pass, and then comes a third announcement. Almost as soon as the agent starts speaking, people are standing up and edging their way towards the desk. A group of a dozen or so hopefuls are now congregating at a barely respectable distance from the target. This time, the sum offered is judged to be worth the disruption to people's schedules. In an instant, there is a mad rush to the desk as traditional Nordic calm and phlegm is abandoned. A lucky handful of would-be travellers gleefully pocket some hard cash, leaving embarrassed losers, including me, skulking back to their seats.

It was all rather unseemly.

I witnessed a similar spectacle at Hong Kong in the 1990s, when I became the unwitting victim of the massive failure of an overbooking forecast. Despite holding a business-class ticket and confirmed reservation I was informed that the overnight flight to Europe was severely overbooked and I was going nowhere that evening. The fact that the airline paid the bills and offered modest compensation could never erase the bad feeling generated. For weeks afterwards I gleefully urged my colleagues to avoid this particular airline and, to this day, I harbour a simmering resentment.

My friend Louis Busuttil would doubtless remind me that the inconvenience I suffered was just bad luck and that I should be grateful that most of the time the practice of overbooking works well enough to ensure that my travel costs are lower than they might otherwise be. I know he is right, but that is little consolation if you happen to be the one who is stranded in Hong Kong on a hot and sultry night.

Jim Barlow of Sabre Airline Solutions is quick to point out that involuntary denied boarding is rare: 'Paradoxically, this is not a good example of bad practice because airlines do it in such a way that the experience ends up being relatively positive.' Inducing customers to self-select, through the offer of vouchers and other incentives, can go a long way to neutralising the fall-out and turn the transaction into a voluntary one.

Fortunately, a set of regulations and guidelines are in force to protect consumer rights concerning denied boarding, cancellations and delays (Aviation Consumer Protection and Enforcement, 2009; European Commission Mobility & Transport 2009).

Fares Fair

The true 'dark side' is nothing to do with revenue management, but everything to do with how airlines communicate their fares to the market. Revenue management is really just a set of procedures to forecast demand and recommend booking limits. We must not bundle revenue management with sleazy or dubious pricing and advertising practices.

First, I will return to the rosy image of airlines showering their loyal customers with offers of free flights. The truth is that 'free' flights are nothing of the sort. Airlines have been gradually increasing the number of miles required for a given flight, as well as imposing charges for requesting flights at short notice, processing the reservation, changing the reservation, reactivating mileage in the event of a cancellation of reservation, or providing a confirmed seat on same-day stand-by. In addition there are taxes, passenger facility and security charges, and fuel surcharges. And if you travel with an infant on your lap, there is yet another fee. Not all airlines impose such charges, and Southwest Airlines is noticeably lenient, but it is no exaggeration to say that special deals, available to anyone, can be less expensive than using up miles on a so-called free flight.

Second, there is no doubt that ticket prices are not always communicated clearly. We all know what it feels like to have paid US$1,200 for ticket and find that the person sitting next to us on the aircraft has paid US$99. We have all had the experience of seeing the US$600 fare that we coveted suddenly jump to US$800 overnight, for no apparent reason. The experts agree that airlines have not done a good job of explaining revenue management to customers. 'I'm not even sure they could if they tried,' quipped Peter Belobaba. The problem is compounded by blatant advertising of low fares without really explaining clearly enough that such fares may have limited availability. Says Belobaba, 'Of course consumers get frustrated when they call up and want to go at five o'clock on Friday and the price is not US$99 but US$700.' In their defence, airlines will argue that restrictions are clearly apparent in the small text but, frankly, they could head off a great deal of unnecessary antagonism if they were to present the offer in a clearer fashion. Jim Barlow concedes that many travellers do not even realise that airlines have sophisticated revenue optimisation systems: 'All they do is observe which fares are available and that seems quite confusing.'

Third, there is the related issue of transparency. The good news for the consumer is that the Internet has blessed the market with the opportunity to visualise a huge array of prices offered by competing airlines. It can even be argued that a consequence of Internet fare transparency has been to pull yields down as the imperative to remain price-competitive has sharpened. This is obviously to the benefit of consumers rather than airlines. However, is the airline industry in good company if we compare pricing transparency in other types of business? Dr Peter Belobaba points at hotels and car hire companies that are, he opines, 'outrageous manipulators of price and capacity. Hotels have all the prices and they won't tell you what they are.' There is even an argument that airlines have gone too far the other way and have given customers too much, rather than too little, visibility. Belobaba's analogy is that if you decide to buy a pair of shoes in a department store you would not expect to have instant visibility on the price of that particular brand of shoe in every other store in the city, so why should travellers expect the same thing with airlines? Somehow, while other industries' track record is hardly impeccable, airlines have offended their customers and must bear the brunt of their outrage.

Fourth, the Internet is well-populated with blogs and sites that discuss the phenomenon of *à la carte* pricing, also referred to as discretionary or even 'hidden' fees. These include charges for making reservations in person, checking in luggage, getting refunds, extra seat pitch or seat assignments. Ryanair vehemently denies that it has hidden charges, but has controversially suggested that charging to use onboard lavatories is a serious option. You have to admit that Michael O'Leary has a point when he says that travellers are happy to pay to access public conveniences in Liverpool Street Station, so should get used to the idea of doing so on board an aircraft (BBC 2009). Perhaps he has not considered the possibility that passengers might limit their purchase of onboard drinks in order to avoid spending the proverbial penny.

One of these so-called hidden fees concerns fuel surcharging. During 2008, when fuel prices shot to an all-time high, airlines legitimately complained about the burden of the uncontrolled escalation of one of their key cost items, yet remained more muted when it came to admitting that they were able to pass a good proportion of these cost increases on to the shoulders of their passengers. Certainly, fuel surcharges reached ridiculous proportions. As an example, a passenger seduced by SpiceJet's 'new special fare' for its daily flight from Mumbai to Hyderabad on 15 July 2009, returning four days later, would have discovered a fuel surcharge equivalent to more than six times the value of the return leg (SpiceJet 2009). At least SpiceJet was clearly stating the fuel surcharge and presented information in a clear and informative manner. Belobaba's reaction to fuel surcharges is vocal: 'A fuel surcharge is ridiculous. Fuel costs are part of your costs of doing business and in my mind there is no difference between charging a fuel surcharge and charging a pilot surcharge when the airline has just reached an agreement with pilots that's costing more money. What kind of nonsense is that?' Quite.

The Internet is awash with horror stories about pricing dishonesty, and user groups are always ready to stand up and defend consumer rights. Needless to say, the press is usually happy to side with the victimised consumer. Then again, discretionary revenue is entirely laudable so long as it is honestly presented and contributes to reducing the overall cost of air travel. Things turn nasty only when passengers either feel that the airline has been holding back clear information about pricing or when they have no option but to pay, as in the case of surcharges and taxes.

Occasionally, the shots are fired from outside the airline industry. For example, Eurostar has proudly claimed that it always advertises the full price and does not 'try to pull the wool over customers' eyes' by advertising a price before taxes and charges are added (Eurostar 2005). The UK Air Transport Users

Council issued a report in 2005, updated in 2007 (AUC 2005, 2007), pointing the finger at airlines that habitually impose taxes, fees and charges that vary wildly on identical routes.

I certainly do not blame airlines for finding new ways to generate revenue, but the challenge they face is that many passengers react negatively when asked to pay for something that they had previously taken for granted as free. The media simply fuels the suspicion. Just as we saw in Chapter 3, passenger expectations need to be better understood and modified if these new charging strategies are to avoid alienating passengers. It was the airline booking companies that fired the first salvo in exposing the effect of the full range of extra charges. TripAdvisor, an online booking company owned by Expedia, introduced a 'fee estimator' in 2009 that provides estimates on fees for in-flight meals and baggage. The giant global distribution systems, Sabre and Amadeus, are planning to unveil their own tools that will give customers a clearer picture of how much they are being charged (McCartney 2009). One airline that has rattled a few cages is British Airways, which unveiled its 'value calculator' on its website in June 2009. This useful tool enables any visitor to its site to compare the overall cost of travel between British Airways, Ryanair and easyJet. The default values of its sample comparative table unsurprisingly reveal that, when the complete range of extra charges is applied, the low-cost carriers end up being more expensive than British Airways (British Airways 2009). However, a random sample of the pricing strategy of British Airways, easyJet and Ryanair reveals very typical pricing behaviour and a more realistic view.

Figure 5.1 shows how airlines manage their pricing in a competitive market. From 8 July 2009 I started keeping a record of the cheapest prices offered by the three airlines for a return journey from London to Toulouse two months hence. It should be noted that British Airways and easyJet compete directly on the Gatwick to Toulouse route, whereas Ryanair connect the cities by using Stansted and Carcassonne airports, the latter being around 100 kilometres from Toulouse. So, it is fair to point out that the markets may not be strictly comparable. Also, British Airways will fill its capacity with connecting traffic, which may be expected to affect pricing decisions on remaining capacity for point-to-point traffic. The values in the chart include fees and taxes, plus the

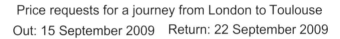

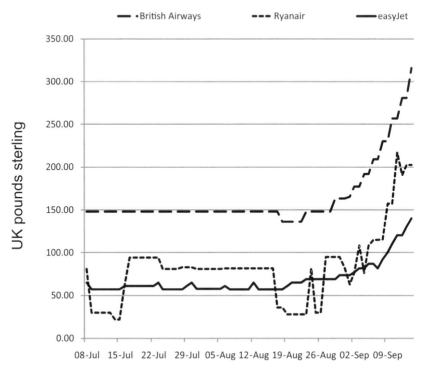

Figure 5.1   A merry dance

Source: Data from British Airways, Ryanair and easyJet websites.

charges levied by the low-cost carriers for a single bag in each direction. For a period of almost six weeks British Airways did not even take the trouble to alter their lowest price which, rather boringly, remained rooted to the spot. Ryanair performed an early pirouette around easyJet in the first week of the analysis period. I would have considered myself unlucky to have checked the pricing on 15 July (£22.00) only to have returned to the site two days later to make a booking (£94.22). In fact, Ryanair's final price for most of July and August mostly comprised fees, online check-in and baggage charges. For long periods, their headline travel price was as low as £1, or even zero in one direction only. On the other hand, easyJet, was far more consistent. About three weeks before the departure of the outward flight all three airlines began to raise prices at a similar pace, although Ryanair was alternately exciting and confusing its market by performing daring quick-steps in final price. The crescendo of this merry dance saw all three performers push pricing upwards as capacity filled in the final days of the flights' life-cycles. Indeed, Ryanair's offer shot up to within striking distance of British Airways for a brief moment, before settling back to occupy mid-stage. Ultimately, however, easyJet completed the dance with the lowest price by a considerable margin.

The ratio of highest price to lowest price within the analysis period is shown in Figure 5.2. British Airways and easyJet manipulated pricing to approximately the same degree. Ryanair, on the other hand, varied pricing within a factor of ten to one. At least the low-cost carriers lived up to expectations of being low-fare – despite what British Airways might want us to believe through its 'value calculator' – although a price-conscious traveller would only realistically nail down the best fare by diligent and regular research into the airlines' antics, combined with a fair slice of luck.

Price requests for a journey from London to Toulouse
Out: 15 September 2009 Return: 22 September 2009

	Highest UK pounds	Lowest UK pounds	High:Low ratio
British Airways	316.00	136.00	2.32
Ryanair	217.16	22.00	9.87
easyJet	139.92	56.83	2.46

Figure 5.2   Pricing ratios
Source: Data from British Airways, Ryanair and easyJet websites.

I'm Looking Through You

The analysis of real pricing on the London to Toulouse route reveals the pitfalls that await the unwary. Independent consumer guidance, such as that available through TripAdvisor, will go some way to mitigating criticism, but until such systems become commonplace and until standards are applied, the price-conscious consumer will continue to feel cheated. Another vivid example, and one which attracted some attention at the time, was Etihad Airways' cheap fares promotion of May 2009, in which a series of enticing deals was published in an e-mail campaign covering destinations in the Middle East and London (Sambridge 2009). Certainly, a US$54 return flight from Abu Dhabi to London was going to attract a lot of attention. To be fair to Etihad, the offer did state that the promotional price did not include surcharges and taxes. The problem arose when prospective passengers discovered, at the end of the online booking process, that the final price was almost seven times the promotional price once the surcharges and taxes had been added. Ironically, the final price was still a reasonable deal, but the passengers felt that the offer was misleading. One budget carrier in the region, Kuwait-based Jazeera Airways, simultaneously offered a headline one-way fare of only US$17 to several destinations, including all taxes and additional fees. Obviously Etihad and Jazeera are not in the same market, but perception is easily swayed by the critical reaction of the press to the Etihad promotion and the rather more positive coverage of Jazeera.

The European Commission can be applauded for launching 'sweeps' of airline websites to check compliance with consumer protection laws, and then naming the perpetrators of misleading behaviour. A report published on 8 May 2008 revealed that 137 of 386 websites investigated were in breach of EU consumer law (EurActiv 2009). Most of these sites were accused of misleading pricing. By May 2009 the EU Consumer Commissioner, Meglena Kuneva, was able to announce that the majority of the offending websites had been corrected (Kuneva 2009). Pricing transparency is an obligation under air services regulation.

The Future of Revenue Management and Pricing

Revenue management has turned into a competitive necessity and is no longer a competitive advantage. Over time the gap between airlines that do a good job at revenue management and those starting out is certain to close. Jim Barlow of Sabre Airline Solutions anticipates a shift towards real-time revenue management. Today, most airlines reset their controls once a night and make ad hoc changes throughout the day. However, in the future we may see a continuous setting of controls to match changes in the selling environment. Thus, when a competitor issues a new fare, or changes a schedule, then the revenue management system will instantly be updated. In some environments booking behaviour is so dynamic that it is just not possible to wait until nightfall to update the system. In India, for example, it is common for bookings to be made in a scramble over the final few days before departure, so real-time revenue management becomes worthwhile.

Sabre periodically examines the value of revenue management to an airline by undertaking an exercise called revenue opportunity modelling. The exercise derives three values, only one of which is known. The known value is the revenue actually achieved by an airline. The second value is an estimate of what *would* have happened had the airline exercised perfect revenue management, and the third value is an estimate of revenue in a situation where revenue management would have been completely absent. Most studies reveal that airlines achieve only about 60 per cent of their revenue potential, leaving a significant opportunity to be exploited. Of course, no airline will ever be able to recapture all of the remaining 40 per cent, but it is clear that we are far from exhausting the possibilities.

The initial wave of revenue management systems was designed in an era of traditional, restricted fare structures. However, pricing practice has since undergone huge change, with the simplified approach of the low-cost carriers blending with the complexities of *à la carte* pricing, and fares based on differentiated products. The problem facing airlines is to keep adapting to new pricing environments, despite the huge investments they have already made in their existing systems.

As future revenue management systems become more dynamic in nature, more sophisticated and more focused on the individual, it is possible that transparency will ironically evaporate. MIT's Dr Peter Belobaba sees no downside in such a development: 'I don't think that transparency is the goal of the airlines. If I'm running an airline I want to make sure that I'm giving my passengers a fair deal and that they are paying what they are willing to pay.

It's not in my interests to make sure that everybody has complete information.'

In Conclusion

Revenue management is undoubtedly a Very Good Thing. It has brought enormous benefits to the industry, although airlines have not done a great job in explaining how revenue management works to the benefit of all passengers. The bigger problem is pricing practice, and in particular how prices are communicated to the market. Confusing pricing strategies and allegations of hidden charges are doing no favours to beleaguered airlines. However, many airlines have been slow to move to clean up dubious practices, leading to regulatory intervention and unwelcome bad publicity. The industry needs to work towards more, rather than less, transparency. Unless moves are made to rectify the bad image of airline pricing, the industry will continue to be unfairly tainted.

References

AUC, 2005. *Taxes, Fees and Charges: An AUC on Pricing on Airlines' Websites*. 25 March. Available at: http://www.auc.org.uk/docs/306/taxes,%20fees%20and%20charges.pdf (accessed 15 September 2009).

AUC, 2007. *Taxes, Fees and Charges: Follow Up Report to 2005 AUC Report on Pricing on Airline Websites*. 4 May. Available at: http://www.auc.org.uk/docs/306/TFC%20press%20release.pdf (accessed 15 September 2009).

Aviation Consumer Protection and Enforcement, US Department of Transportation, 2009. *Fly-Rights: A Consumer Guide to Air Travel*. Available at: http://airconsumer.dot.gov/publications/flyrights.htm (accessed 20 December 2009).

BBC, 2009. 'Ryanair Mulls Charge for Toilets'. 27 February. Available at: http://news.bbc.co.uk/2/hi/business/7914542.stm (accessed 20 December 2009).

British Airways, 2009. 'BA Value Calculator'. Available at: http://www.britishairways.com/travel/value-calculator/public/en_gb (accessed 15 December 2009).

EurActiv.com, 2009. 'Commission Urges End to Air Ticket Price "Rip-offs"' 15 May. Available at: http://www.euractiv.com/en/transport/commission-urges-air-ticket-price-rip-offs/article-182387 (accessed 20 December 2009).

European Commission Mobility & Transport, 2009. 'Passenger Rights'. Available at: http://ec.europa.eu/transport/passengers/index_en.htm (accessed 20 December 2009).

Eurostar, 2005. 'Eurostar Criticizes Airline Pricing Dishonesty'. 23 March. Available at: http://www.eurostar.com/UK/uk/leisure/about_eurostar/ press_release/press_archive_2005/23_03_05.jsp (accessed 20 December 2009).

Hess, C.A., 1998. 'If Airlines Sold Paint'. © Alan H. Hess 1998. All rights reserved. Printed with permission.

Kuneva, M., 2009. 'Consumers: Airlines Move to Clean up Ticket Selling Websites'. Press release, 14 May. Available at: http://ec.europa.eu/ commission_barroso/kuneva/press_en.htm (accessed 14 May 2009).

McCartney, S., 2009. 'Airfare Quotes That Lay Bare Hidden Fees'. 10 March. Available at: http://online.wsj.com/article/SB123664662318478683.html (accessed 10 March 2009).

Sambidge, A. 2009. 'Etihad Launches $54 Return Flights to Heathrow'. 4 May. Available at: http://www.arabianbusiness.com/554522 (accessed 4 June 2009).

SpiceJet, 2009. SpiceJet Booking Zone. Available at: http://book.spicejet.com/ skylights/cgi-bin/skylights.cgi (accessed 15 July 2009).

Chapter 6

'With a Little Help From My Friends': Social Media

Channels of human interaction and communication are in the process of undergoing an astounding revolution. Airlines are being presented with new opportunities to connect with their markets in ways that were unimaginable just a couple of years ago. Unless airlines get a better grip on new communications technologies they will run ever-increasing risks that their brands will come under powerful attack from individuals who quickly harness and exploit social media and its ready audience. It is to this phenomenon that we now turn.

Welcome to the Social Media Juggernaut

The term 'social media' means different things to different people, so it is as well to start the discussion with a definition appropriate to the context.

Social media is a form of organic conversation involving the distribution of content that is generated and controlled by individuals, circulating freely by physical, electronic or verbal means, and where comment and feedback by the community is encouraged. Social media is arguably the ultimate democracy of expression, typified by e-mails, blogs, podcasts, video- and photo-sharing, voice-over IP, message forums and boards, and wikis. The expression 'user-generated content' is sometimes alternatively applied by the business community.

At first glance, social media may appear to have a lot in common with traditional mass media. For example, both types are accessible to potentially vast audiences. But there are key differences that have significant implications for how knowledge, information and opinion are disseminated. First, unlike traditional broadcast or print media, social media requires no specialist skill or knowledge and is readily available at reasonable cost. Second, social media is ephemeral in nature, and can be rapidly generated, altered and deleted, leaving less of a trace than traditional media. Third, social media has an immediacy that traditional media lacks. Thus, it was possible for a ferryboat passenger to upload, to the Twitter microblogging site, information and photographs concerning the US Airways A320 ditching in the Hudson River a matter of minutes after the actual occurrence and well before traditional media had a chance to react (Deards 2009). Another Twitter user broke the story of a Turkish Airlines 737-800 accident at Schiphol (Chowdhry 2009). Even more amazing was the story of Continental Airlines passenger Mike Wilson, who was on a 737 that overran the runway in Denver. Wilson actually updated the Twitter community on what was happening during the incident itself (Mackey 2008).

Indeed, the rapid rise of the Twitter phenomenon raises questions about the sometimes uncomfortable relationship between professional and citizen journalists. Naturally, professional journalists argue that they are trained to be impartial, that they apply rigorous ethical standards and possess the ability to write eloquently and to the highest standard. Equally naturally, citizen journalists point to the democratisation of news dissemination brought about by the Internet and their ability to generate community involvement by using the growing array of social media tools. One thing is certain. Heaping scorn on citizen journalists and social media will not slow the development of the phenomenon. Social media is here to stay, so we had better get used to it. The key for businesses looking to extract some advantage from this form of communication is to distinguish between users who spend their time telling each other when they are shampooing their hair or walking their dogs, and users who have a serious interest in interacting with organisations with which they spend their cash. As already pointed out, it is the community at large, or customers, who are populating the social media sites with content, so it is just as well that an organisation exerts some control of that content before the content starts to control the organisation. The question for management is one of how best to embrace the opportunities offered up by technology.

Developing a strategy for social media is an absolute 'must', rather than rushing to establish various tools just for the sake of it. A strategy should address the precise areas that have relevancy for the business and must reinforce the brand, so let's take a look at some examples.

One common social media objective for an airline or airport operator is to pass on information about flight delays. Another objective would be to promote special offers. In this case, offers may even be limited to users of social media, as a means of encouraging its adoption. Another marketing-related objective would be to use social media to drive traffic to the company website and generate new sales leads, although some channels might limit the degree to which this is possible.

Bearing in mind the growing ubiquity of social media and its all-encompassing nature, it makes sense to use it to form a relationship with customers as far as possible, and it should be no surprise that engagement is what customers expect. The whole purpose of these tools is to get communication going, and that means in both directions. Resources must be in place to deal with a potential onslaught of questions that may require rapid action. After all, these tools are an easy way of finding out what is going on, even if comments may be both negative and complimentary. Being alerted to a problem by following a Twitter exchange presents an opportunity to grab the initiative and address the issue before it becomes a crisis.

Should every airline open a Twitter account and Facebook page? Not at all. Just because it seems to be the flavour of the moment does not mean that it is always the best way of supporting the brand. First, it is important to match the method of communication to the target market. If a particular market is not connected to the blogosphere, then social media may not be the best way forward. You would not be surprised to learn that it is the younger, technology-savvy generation that is most likely to be found using social media. There is, however, a difference in behaviour between Generation X (those born between the mid-1960s and the end of the 1970s) and Generation Y (those born between 1980 and the mid-1990s). Generation Xers consider technology as a vital means to support their lifestyle needs, such as shopping and banking, for example. Generation Y uses computers just as much as their elder cousins, but, importantly, considers computers as virtually embedded into all of their activities. Generation Y is considered as the first native online population (Ferguson 2009). As Generation Y matures and wealth grows, this segment will become an increasingly significant group with high travel propensity, so building a long-term relationship with Generation Y should begin right now. Future air travellers will also come from the grouping known as Generation Z, being those born from the mid-1990s onwards. Already, this population is highly motivated by social media, and we can expect the emergence of a new market segment with completely different expectations in terms of how they communicate with airlines.

Surprisingly, despite strong evidence that social media is more than just a passing fad, professional marketers appear to harbour misgivings. A 2009 survey conducted by Anderson Analytics for the Marketing Executives Networking Group revealed that two-thirds of executive marketers still consider themselves novices when it comes to using social media for marketing purposes. Furthermore, twice as many marketers confessed to being 'sick' of hearing about social networking and other buzzwords than in the previous year's survey (MENG 2009). So, does this suggest that marketing professionals are reminiscent of the Luddites, readying their axes to smash the new-fangled technology? Or do they believe that the social media phenomenon is a flash in the pan?

The figures suggest otherwise. At the time of writing (March 2010), the total number of active users of Facebook amounted to a massive 400 million. The top 33 sites have followers equivalent in number the population of the United Kingdom. Indeed, if Facebook were a country it would rank as the world's fourth largest, between the United States and Indonesia. Social media is not limited to the Western world, however. China's QZone is rumoured to have over 300 million users, and Russia may well boast the world's largest social media audience of all (Qualman 2009).

It is encouraging that a significant number of airlines have thrown themselves headlong into the open arms of social media. As of August 2009, of the top 100 airlines as measured by revenue, no less than 54 had signed up to Twitter and 65 operated a

Facebook page. Doubtless the number of airlines jumping on the social media bandwagon will continue to increase.

However, there is a gigantic disparity between two airlines that have clearly made a great success of their foray into social media and the rest of the Twitter and Facebook adopters. As of June 2010 JetBlue Airways could boast over 1.6 million Twitter followers and Southwest Airlines over 1 million. The Virgin founder, Sir Richard Branson, has a personal Twitter account with 380,000 followers, but the next airline on the list is United Airlines, with 88,000 followers, occupying a lowly global ranking position of only 1,755th. United is closely followed, incidentally, by Virgin America, with 86,000 followers. The vast majority of airlines hardly make a dent in the rankings. To put United Airlines' achievement as the third-ranking airline into perspective, consider the Twitter position of the person purporting to be rock musician David Bowie. For several years his membership tally managed to keep pace with that of United Airlines, but with rather less effort. In fact, he has only ever posted a single 'tweet', to the effect that the weather in Berlin was snowy and that he was working on 'new material'. Incredibly, despite David Bowie's apparent reluctance to communicate, his faithful followers are nevertheless increasing at an average rate of up to 26 per day (TwitterCounter 2010a). This puts the phenomenon of social media into an interesting perspective. The most popular sites are those belonging to celebrities, media professionals and the more colourful of our politicians. Nevertheless, JetBlue Airways and Southwest Airlines have managed to break the mould by carving an astonishingly powerful position in a potentially golden market. So, it can be done.

Christi Day is responsible for emerging media at Southwest and has a clear idea of why her airline is so successful with the new technology: 'It goes back to the Southwest way. Our customers expect us to be different, to become the maverick, and to lead the industry.' According to Christi, this culture can be communicated through the use of social media, such as YouTube, Facebook and Twitter. And Southwest's customers are particularly receptive to this form of communication. Says Christi, 'Within the next five years, it will become second nature for people to Twitter, to Facebook, to blog, because that's the kind of interaction they're wanting.' Southwest Airlines, it must be admitted, had the good fortune to be added, in June 2009, to Twitter's list of recommended sites to follow. These recommended sites are typically those where people tweet often and include relevant information in their tweets. Once Southwest made it on to this list, the growth of followers rocketed.

Christi Day is convinced that social media is no longer a fad: 'We are in the middle of a huge revolution that's happening in all forms of communication. It's definitely where business is going and, as a company, it is definitely wise to shape your messages in that way.' Many airlines will agree with Christi. Both American Airlines and Virgin America use Facebook as an alternative booking platform. In the case of Virgin America, customers can search flights, check flight status and post customer reviews.

Some airlines have set up specific websites in order to engage with specific market segments. For example, both AirTran and Lufthansa have sites dedicated to the student population, and KLM has launched social networks dedicated to particular markets, such as KLM Club China and KLM Club Africa. Another twist is to target special-interest groups, which KLM has done with its Flying Blue Golf site. One of the more unusual social networking sites is one established by SAS aimed at the high-income gay, lesbian bisexual and transsexual community.

Another way in which airlines are connecting with their customers is through iPhone applications, to allow boarding pass retrieval, flight status and other alerts. Among the airlines going down this path are Qantas, American Airlines and Air Canada.

Unsurprisingly, airlines have made judicious use of YouTube to garner publicity. There are plenty of innovative boarding announcement videos to be found, but perhaps the most unusual was Air New Zealand's two 'Nothing to Hide' promotional videos, featuring a team of nude, but body-painted, Air New Zealand staff, including the Chief Executive Officer himself, Rob Fyfe, who sportingly played a baggage handler. Combined viewing hits of the two videos exceeded 8 million by September 2009. The campaign was intended to convey the message that Air New Zealand was not applying hidden charges in their fares. The astonishingly positive media and public reaction to the two videos undoubtedly boosted Air New Zealand's brand.

The Sting in the Tail

Before we get carried away with the idea that social media is on the verge of becoming the predominant means of communications in the future, we should take a step back and look at some disturbing realities. An investigation by global researcher Synovate in 2008 found that in the 17 markets and 13,000 people surveyed, 58 per cent of respondents did not know what social networking was, and that over one-third of social networkers were losing interest. This was admittedly partly the result of the wide age groups surveyed. The survey revealed that one of the greatest fears expressed by people using social media was the risk of identity fraud and risk of being accused of posting defamatory content. More than half of those surveyed considered that language skills were deteriorating as a result of online social networking. Perhaps even more telling was the discovery that in some markets, such as South Africa, Taiwan and the United Arab Emirates, around one-third of respondents admitted that they had more friends online than in the 'real' world (Synovate 2008).

There is some more bad news for advertisers on social media sites as well. A report issued by LinkedIn Research Network and Harris Interactive suggested that only 8 per cent of both Internet users and advertisers in the United States felt that Twitter was a very effective platform for promoting products and ideas (Social Media 2009).

Flight International magazine posed a 'Question of the week' in May 2009, asking readers to nominate their favourite means of keeping abreast of aviation. Almost 90 per cent of those polled gave 'online news' or 'magazines' as their preferred means. That left 6 per cent favouring discussion forums, just 4 per cent reading blogs, and a paltry 1 per cent using Twitter to get their aviation news (Flightglobal 2009). Of course, those involved in this particular poll were largely people working within the aerospace industry in general rather than airline customers, where we might expect the numbers to be somewhat different. Yet easyJet, which carried 45.2 million passengers in 2009, could boast a grand total of only 6,244 followers of their @easyjetcare Twitter service as at March 2010 (TwitterCounter 2010b). That equates to 0.00014 per cent of their actual market. JetBlue's Twitter penetration,

Based on 22.45 million passengers carried in 2009, is 7 per cent (TwitterCounter 2010c). JetBlue, along with Southwest Airlines, is definitely showing everyone else what can be achieved, but these statistics do rather put things into perspective. Even the irrepressible Christi Day of Southwest is quick to acknowledge that, despite the success of social media, the numbers represent just a 'drop in the bucket' in relation to the total number of passengers carried.

One problem that constantly arises is that passengers tend to use microblogging sites like Twitter, as well as Facebook, as channels to air their grievances. For airlines using social media as customer service tools this has important implications. It is estimated that one-third of all bloggers post opinions about products and services, and that 78 per cent of consumers trust peer recommendations (Qualman 2009). Furthermore, 80 per cent of Twitter usage is on mobile devices. The combined effect results in a potent cocktail of opportunity as well as threat. A bad customer service experience, or a delayed flight, could easily act as a catalyst for a weary traveller to pull out a mobile device and promptly share his or her thoughts with, literally, a vast and impressionable audience. An example of just how easily things spiral out of hand befell South African Airways. Television presenter Richard Quest became frustrated when his flight from Cape Town to Johannesburg was delayed, blaming SAA for what turned out to be adverse weather conditions beyond the control of the airline. Quest's reaction was to 'tweet' his views on the situation to his followers, numbering more than 23,000 in March 2010. South African Airways defended itself admirably, but the damage had already been done (Quest 2009).

Indeed, a significant number of comments made by members of social media sites are critical rather than supportive. Even the most innocuous videos posted on YouTube seem to attract comments that escalate into vicious rants and personal attacks. A travel opinion website has referred to Twitter as 'an underground rage factory' (Peterson 2009). Southwest's Christi Day retorts that such a description is 'completely off the mark' and that her airline's experience is quite the opposite. EasyJet has even borne an attack from a disgruntled traveller who has set up what can only be described as a hate site, with the objective of spreading negative comment about the airline. The use of a segment of the easyJet logo in the identification of this particular site is an example of 'brandjacking', where a logo or image is used in an inappropriate manner. Indeed, Twitter is awash with phoney accounts set up by individuals who assume the identity of celebrities. Nevertheless, easyJet's own foray into social media has seemed rather half-hearted, it must be said. Its Twitter site is bravely managed by a dedicated individual but, with just over 1,200 followers, the airline is only putting a toe in the water.

At least easyJet is making an effort to connect with its customers. Rival carrier Ryanair has abandoned Twitter after a brandjacking incident in which an individual set up a bogus site directing abusive comments towards Ryanair and its passengers (Keenan 2009).

Sometimes, the problems can emanate from within the organisation itself. A group of British Airways ground staff created a Facebook page that criticised passengers as well as the airline's handling of the opening of Terminal 5 at London's Heathrow airport (Millward 2008).

One of the most embarrassing Twitter posts took place when an executive of Ketchum, a public relations agency, shared with his followers some unflattering comments about the city of Memphis, home of FedEx. To make matters worse, the 'tweet' was posted on the very day that he was meeting a group of FedEx managers in order to make a presentation on the subject of digital media. One recipient of the 'tweet' brought it to the attention of FedEx who, as proud citizens of Memphis, were somewhat offended. It is hard to imagine a worse example of an own goal. Although no offence was intended, and an apology quickly followed, this serves as a sobering example of the hazards of writing down one's personal thoughts and then broadcasting them to the world.

Perhaps the most colourful example to date of the power of social media concerns the experience of a Canadian musician named Dave Carroll and his band 'Sons of Maxwell'.

'United Breaks Guitars'

Dave Carroll and his fellow musicians had changed aircraft in Chicago, having checked their instruments through to their final destination. The band had boarded its United Airlines connecting flight and was awaiting departure. Dave takes up the story:

> A woman sitting on the baggage loading side cried out, 'Oh my God, they're throwing guitars outside!' We all had a sick feeling in our stomachs. I tried to engage the flight attendant when everyone left the plane. She put her hand up in my face and said, 'Don't talk to me, talk to the lead agent.' I tried to talk to that person and she ran up the gangway saying she was not the lead agent. I talked to a person at the gate and she stopped me and said, 'But, hun, that's why you sign the waiver,' as though there's some piece of paper that everyone in the world signs that excuses that kind of behaviour.

But that was only the start of Dave Carroll's problems. The object that sustains his livelihood, a Taylor guitar, had indeed been damaged as a result of being thrown by a baggage handler. Everyone who Carroll talked to in United Airlines either did not care or did not care to do anything about the situation. Months passed and United refused to pay compensation or even apologise. Dave Carroll realised that, as a songwriter and musician, he could create an opportunity to force United's hand. Dave even told the airline of his intention to write three songs and produce three videos on YouTube about the experience.

True to his word, the first song and video, *United Breaks Guitars*, was uploaded with little fanfare on 6 July 2009. Says Dave:

> The next morning I looked on YouTube and there were 300 hits. I was ecstatic because I was worried that no-one would look at it. I thought that 300 is not a bad start.

That was an understatement. Within just two days, *United Breaks Guitars* had been viewed by 135,000 times. Just two days later the number was 1.7 million. Almost immediately the mainstream media noticed, and stories appeared on prime news sites and broadcasts throughout North America, which served to further fuel the visits to YouTube. But the story was also being promulgated by other social media, such as blogs and Twitter. Between 6 July and 8 July the story was told in approximately 339 mainstream online news sites and featured in well over 700 blogs. When the story began to appear in European media on 23 July, the number of YouTube views peaked at 180,000 per day. For the month of July 2009 *United Breaks Guitars* boasted over 4.5 million views (Serjeantson 2009).

United Breaks Guitars is a near-perfect illustration of how an individual can rapidly harness the extraordinary power of a social media channel and attract the attention of a number of media watchers, who have tried to make sense of what happened. First, it seems that the viral nature of the growth of the story was not exclusively in the hands of social media, but was spread across the spectrum of media. Analysis by MediaMiser, a media consulting organisation, suggests that mainstream media's reporting of the story had a greater influence on Twitter than Twitter had on the mainstream media. For example, almost all of the embedded links in tweets referenced mainstream online publications. However, the primary influencers in propelling the story forward appeared to have come from the blogosphere, rather than traditional outlets.

A second outcome was that United Airlines was rendered powerless in controlling the outpouring of comment, mostly negative, about the airline and the industry's perceived poor performance in customer service. The airline quickly announced that it would like to use the video for internal training purposes, but damage control seemed to be an insurmountable challenge at the time. For example, it was reported that United Airlines' share price had 'plunged' by 10 per cent, wiping US$180 million off the company's value (BBC 2009). However, the reality was somewhat different. On the day that the share price story appeared, 22 July, the share price indeed dropped by 10 per cent from US$3.72 to US$3.36, but within two days the shares had rebounded to US$3.79 (MarketWatch 2009). These swings were well within normal fluctuations, so it is not true that Dave Carroll had single-handedly reduced the value of United Airlines. Nevertheless, a breakdown of the top United Airlines issues discussed in online news reveals that *United Breaks Guitars* accounted for 42 per cent of news activity (Serjeantson 2009). Incidentally, United's share price had reached US$11 on 15 December 2009, so no lasting damage had been done.

Has United Airlines learned a lesson? Dave Carroll is not particularly sanguine when it comes to answering that question. 'I'm not sure that they're learning anything,' says Dave, who remains unconvinced that airlines are able to render adequate service when it comes to transporting their customers' property.

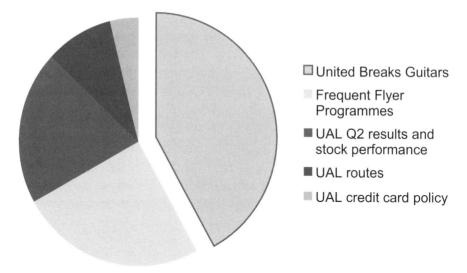

Figure 6.1   Top United Airlines news issues, July 2009
Source: Serjeantson (2009).

Probably the most significant outcome of the *United Breaks Guitars* story concerns the support he has given to another group of disenchanted air travellers who are pushing for legislation for passenger rights.

In Conclusion

Competition will become ever sharper in the airline business and, in markets where the product can become increasingly commoditised, it makes sense to enhance customer service as much as possible. Social media heralds a complete shift in the way in which people communicate. Like it or not, every paying customer holds the power to either destroy or heap accolades on a brand. A social media strategy, with well-thought-through objectives and a dedicated team, has already become an essential ingredient for protecting and enhancing a brand, and for creating an environment in which every customer feels both valued and welcome. However, even though airlines are establishing their own social media sites, especially Facebook and Twitter, only a small handful have really understood the enormous potential of these new media. The vast majority of airlines are simply failing to jump on the bandwagon.

Despite the apparent benefits, social media sites have the effect of handing communication power to each and every customer, who in turn has a potential audience of millions. Just a single mistake on the part of the airline can result in vast damage to a reputation. Ignoring such sites will not stop their development and will not stop people communicating. Handle with care!

References

BBC, 2007. '"Unlucky" Airline Logo Grounded'. 21 February. Available at: http://news.bbc.co.uk/2/hi/europe/6383171.stm (accessed 15 September 2009).

BBC, 2009. 'Singer's Airline Tune Takes Off' (with video). 23 July. Available at: http://news.bbc.co.uk/2/hi/americas/8164273.stm (accessed 23 July 2009).

Brandchannel, 2006. 'Asia-Pacific Rankings'. Available at: http://www. brandchannel.com/boty_results/asia_list.asp (accessed 20 November 2009).

Chowdhry, A., 2009. 'Twitter Citizen Journalist Jonathan Nipp Reports Plane Crash at Amsterdam Schipol Airport First'. 25 February. Available at: http://pulse2.com/2009/02/25/twitter-citizen-journalist-jonathan-nipp-reports-plane-crash-at-amsterdam-schipol-airport-first/ (accessed 25 September 2009).

Deards, H., 2009. 'Twitter First off the Mark with Hudson Plane Crash Coverage'. 19 January. Available at: http://www.editorsweblog.org/ multimedia/2009/01/twitter_first_off_the_mark_with_hudson_p.php (accessed 20 December 2009).

Ferguson, T., 2008. 'Gen Y is Setting the Tech Agenda'. Available at: www. businessweek.com/globalbiz/content/jul2008/gb20080730_562367.htm (accessed 9 June 2010).

Flightglobal, 2009. 'What's Your Favourite Means of Following Aviation?'. Available at: http://www.flightglobal.com/polls/list.PageID_3.htm (accessed 9 June 2010).

Interbrand, 2009. 'Best Global Brands: 2009 Rankings'. Available at: http://www. interbrand.com/best_global_brands.aspx (accessed 10 October 2009).

Keenan, S., 2009. 'Ryanair Shuts Down Twitter Site'. 5 March. Available at: http://timesonline.co.uk/tol/travel/news/article5851864.ece (accessed 5 March 2009).

Mackay, R., 2008. 'Plane Crash Survivor Tweets the Aftermath'. 22 December. Available at: http://thelede.blogs.nytimes.com/2008/12/22/plane-crash-survivor-tweeets-from-denver (accessed 9 June 2010).

Market Executives Networking Group (MENG), 2009. 'Marketing Executives Networking Group Releases Second Annual Top Marketing Trends for 2009'. 5 January. Available at: http://www.mengonline.com/visitors/news room/ (accessed 11 September 2009).

MarketWatch, 2009. 'MarketWatch News on UAUA'. Available at: http://www.marketwatch.com/investing/stock/uaua/historical (Accessed 9 June 2010).

Millward, D., 2008. 'British Airways Staff Attack Passengers on Facebook'. 2 November. Available at: http://www.telegraph.co.uk/travel/3366187/British-Airways-staff-attack-passengers-on-Facebook.html (accessed 9 September 2009).

Peterson, K., 2009. 'Frustrated Tweets New Headache for Airlines'. Available at: http://www.reuters.com/article/technology/News/idUSTRE57H6E92 0090819 (accessed 22 August 2009).

Qualman, E., 2009. 'Statistics Show Social Media is Bigger than You Think'. 11 August. Available at: http://socialnomics.net/2009/08/11/statistics-show-social-media-is-bigger-than-you-think/ (accessed 6 September 2009).

Quest, R., 2009. 'Tweets from 16 May 2009'. Available at: http://twitter.com/richardquest (accessed 21 September 2009).

Serjeantson, B., 2009. 'United Breaks Guitars Viral Analysis'. Available at: http://www.mediamiser.com/resources/archive/090821_united.html (accessed 15 August 2009).

Social Media, 2009. 'Are Advertisers Cooling on Twitter?' Available at: http://social-media-optimization.com/2009/08/are-advertisers-cooling-on-twitter (accessed 24 May 2010).

Synovate, 2008. 'Global Survey Shows 58% of People Don't Know What Social Networking Is, Plus Over One Third of Social Networkers are Losing Interest'. 1 September. Available at: http://www.synovate.com/news/article/2008/09/global-survey-shows-58-of-people-don-t-know-what-social-networking-is-plus-over-one-third-of-social-networkers-are-losing-interest.html (accessed 1 September 2009).

TwitterCounter, 2010a. 'David Bowie Twitter Statistics'. Available at: http://twittercounter.com/david%20bowie (accessed 11 June 2010).

TwitterCounter, 2010b. 'easyJetCare Twitter Statistics'. Available at: http://twittercounter.com/easyjetcare (accessed 11 June 2010).

TwitterCounter, 2010c. 'JetBlue Twitter Statistics'. Available at: http://twittercounter.com/jetblue (accessed 11 June 2010).

Chapter 7

'Strawberry Fields Forever': The Environment

It is probably true to say that the potent combination of aviation and the environment has aroused more debate, emotion, confusion, extremism, prejudice, jealousy and spitting fury than any other issue that our industry has had to endure in recent times. Whether you believe in human-induced, or anthropogenic, global warming or not, the emission of carbon into the atmosphere is emblematic of the dark side of industrial and technological progress. Any discussion including the dread words 'climate change' is laden with propaganda, politics and many other perils. In short, the environment is a nasty business.

Air transport stands out like a sore thumb as a polluter of our planet, and there's nowhere to hide. In a world where perception is everything, the airline industry is a sitting duck, and an easy target for climate change evangelists to shoot at. Yet, despite the frequent barbs and criticisms hurled at aviation, enormous strides have been made in a remarkably short period to openly address the issues and contain the challenge of being environmentally responsible. In the wake of the failure of the Copenhagen summit on climate change at the end of 2009, we are no closer to an ultimate solution to the problem. Opinions and technical initiatives are moving rapidly; policies and decision-making less so. Rather, this chapter will explore the different positions of the vested interests and attempt to bring some perspective to the overall question of how the airline industry should face up to the almost impossible task of pleasing everybody.

It is important to point out that concern about the environment is not a new phenomenon. Naturalists have been crossing swords with industrialists and economic interests since before the time of Charles Darwin. As early as 1824 a French physicist called

Joseph Fourier was the first to write about the 'greenhouse effect' (Fourier 1824). In 1861 an Irishman named John Tyndall made the connection between water vapour and greenhouse gas noting from his experiments, 'this aqueous vapour is a blanket more necessary to the vegetable life of England than clothing is to man' (Tyndall Centre). Just a few decades later, in 1896, a Nobel Prize-winning Swedish chemist called Svante Arrhenius established that greenhouse gases were driven by the burning of coal (Lycos Retriever).

It was not until the 1960s that the modern environmental movement got under way and the first organised forces squared up not against fossil fuel burners, but against the chemical industry to claim a famous victory by achieving a ban on the insecticide DDT. The establishment of major non-governmental organisations (NGOs), such as Greenpeace and Friends of the Earth in 1971, gave focus to a growing army of concerned individuals and philosophers calling for the value of nature to be recognised. Although these NGOs initially had their plates full in combating whaling and nuclear testing, their focus has gradually shifted to embrace the environmental cause. In the 1980s the term 'sustainable development' was coined, a somewhat amorphous expression quickly adopted as the environmental movement's mantra and inspiration. Twenty years later, virtually every aspect of our lives is touched by the environmental debate. And the biggest debate of all concerns climate change, which has spawned something akin to a fashion industry, complete with a snappy vocabulary ('Are *you* offsetting your carbon footprint?') and plenty of dark undertones suggesting a battle between good and evil.

As aviation is a highly visible activity bearing historically elitist connotations, environmentalists have unsurprisingly used it as a convenient punchbag in order to bring about change and further their own agendas. The problem is that the story keeps changing. Just consider this sample of headlines from the *New York Times* over the last century:

> 10 June 1923: 'Menace of a New Ice Age To Be Tested by Scientists'.
> 20 February 1969: 'Expert Says Arctic Ocean Will Soon Be an Open Sea'.

21 May 1975: 'Scientists Ask Why World Climate Is Changing: Major Cooling May Be Ahead'.
20 May 2005: 'Warming Is Blamed for Antarctica's Weight Gain'.

Doesn't all this look Orwellian? So, we can agree that the battle cry is definitely global warming. Incidentally, the more politically correct term, 'climate change', has largely supplanted the term 'global warming', although it is worth pointing out that the two expressions are not synonymous. Climate change refers to long-term change in the average climate of the planet, whereas global warming concerns a particular *type* of climate change – namely, the warming of the lower atmosphere as a result of an increase in greenhouse gases.

One of the earliest environmental causes involving aviation concerned airport noise, rather than greenhouse gases. The issue of noise was largely overcome by the development of fuel-efficient high-bypass ratio turbofan engines, although it would be a mistake to believe that the issue of aircraft noise has gone away. Noise disturbance of communities neighbouring airports is regularly used as a weapon to combat airport expansion. By the early 1990s the principal buzzword had become 'NO_x', or nitrogen oxides, marking a shift of attention to the potentially destabilising effects on our climate by aircraft. A global, but European-led, data-gathering project in the 1990s called Mosaic, or 'Measurement of Ozone on Airbus In-service Aircraft', never even considered the effect of carbon dioxide on the atmosphere. Then, for a brief time in 2002 climatologists deduced that the grounding of all North American commercial flights from 11 to 14 September 2001 had resulted in an apparent reduction in daily temperature variation of $1°$ Celsius. Perhaps vapour trails were impacting on temperatures? And whatever happened to that hole in the ozone layer? Well, environmentalists will point out that the Montreal Protocol in 1987 set in motion the phasing out of ozone-depleting chemicals, although complete recovery of the ozone layer is not expected for decades.

Past alarms have somehow been either erased from public consciousness or else minimised, to be replaced by the biggest scare of them all: anthropogenic global warming, allegedly induced by the reckless and unfettered emission of that demon greenhouse gas, carbon dioxide, or CO_2. There are numerous beliefs to consider, but I will focus on two principal factions.

In the Red Corner

First, there is a camp convinced that global warming is taking place and that this warming is fuelled by the emission of a number of particulates and gases, but especially carbon dioxide emissions, all greatly exacerbated by human activity, especially aviation. Unless action is taken to arrest the growth in human-induced emissions, this camp believes that catastrophic climate change will occur. It is as well to point out that representatives in governments, NGOs, the environmental pressure groups, the airline industry, IATA and ICAO almost exclusively adhere to, or dare not challenge, this belief. The technical background that largely supports this camp's position can be found in publications of the Intergovernmental Panel on Climate Change (IPCC), a body established in 1988 by the World Meteorological Organisation and the United Nations Environment Programme. The IPCC's role is to assess information in terms of science, technology and socio-economic considerations. The IPCC has developed a specific measure, called 'radiative forcing', expressed as watts per square metre (W/m^2), which takes into account the warming capacity of the atmosphere. For aviation, it is basically the product of various aircraft emissions, especially carbon dioxide, nitrogen oxides and water vapour. The use of radiative forcing in the assessment of aircraft emissions is important because it considers the effect of low temperatures at aircraft cruise altitudes as well as the different ways in which ozone may be affected. So it is not correct, the IPCC argues, to assume that aviation's impact on climate change is limited to carbon emissions alone. Indeed, the IPCC suggests that the total net radiative forcing from aviation is 160 per cent higher than the simple radiative forcing effect of carbon emissions (Whitelegg and Williams 2000). The IPCC believes that by 2050, based on a 'mid-range' growth forecast, the radiative forcing effect of annual aviation emissions could increase by a whopping 700 per cent compared to a 1992 baseline. Put simply, if nothing is done to combat aviation emissions growth, 10 per cent of all anthropogenic radiative forcing would come from aviation by 2050, making aviation the single biggest contributor to climate change.

No wonder people are scared.

And in the Blue Corner

But there is a second faction that adheres to a very different belief. This camp also acknowledges global warming, but believes that this is part of natural cyclical oscillations in the temperature of the planet. The fundamental difference in opinion is that this group believes that carbon emissions, human-induced or otherwise, are a *product* rather than a *driver* of temperature change. The implications of this theory are so dramatic that further explanation is merited.

Planet earth is subject to two sets of temperature oscillation. First, there is a 100,000-year cycle in which the variation is sufficient to induce an ice age (Calder 1974). Embedded within this underlying cycle is a series of shorter timescales of anything between 100 and 1,000 years, during which the oscillation amplitude is less – perhaps just a couple of degrees Celsius. The most recent warm periods were the Roman and medieval periods. We are currently in the 'Modern' warm period, although it is not certain whether current temperatures have surpassed those in previous warm periods. What is certain is that temperatures are indeed rising. Critically, it can be proven that CO_2 oscillations are very much in synchronisation with temperature oscillations. This raises the biggest chicken-and-egg question of all time. Does the warming of the planet drive CO_2 or does CO_2 drive temperature?

Robert Essenhigh, Professor of Energy Conversion at Ohio State University, is one of many proponents of the theory that global warming is not driven by carbon emissions. The central point is that CO_2 from combustion comprises only 5 per cent of the total CO_2 going into the atmosphere. The CO_2 in the atmosphere forms only about 20 per cent of the major greenhouse gases, with the remainder being mostly water. So this puts fossil fuel combustion-induced CO_2 at a very low level: specifically 5 percent of 20 per cent, which is 1 per cent. His paper to the American Chemical Society concluded that the CO_2 contribution to the atmosphere from combustion is so small as to be within the statistical noise of the major sea and vegetation exchanges, and that advocates of the CO_2-driven theory are 'evidently back to front' (Essenhigh 2001). When asked how he felt about the fact that a vast amount of effort being directed at future carbon emission control might be misguided, Professor Essenhigh replied, 'Exasperated. Why don't people look at the numbers? You could double the CO_2 and the atmosphere would hardly blink.'

An atmospheric physicist at the University of Virginia, Dr S. Fred Singer, has said in a letter to the *Wall Street Journal*, 'There is no dispute at all about the fact that even if punctiliously observed, the Kyoto Protocol would have an imperceptible effect on future temperatures: one twentieth of a degree by 2050' (Singer 2001).

If these eminent scientists' conclusions prove to be correct, then it follows that the huge efforts required to induce reductions in CO_2 emissions are unjustified. Indeed, the imposition of all Kyoto CO_2 reductions, equally and in every country in the world, would reduce total human-induced greenhouse contributions from CO_2 by just 0.035 per cent (Geocraft 2003). Essenhigh pulls no punches, asserting, 'Carbon emissions control is totally misdirected and a waste of time and resources to achieve nothing. In view of the expected costs this could wreck our economy.' For environmentalists, conclusions of this nature are, of course, tantamount to heresy.

Astonishingly, proponents of anthropogenic climate change sometimes fail to acknowledge contradictory scientific research. A public climate change conference at McGill University in November 2009 took it as read that CO_2 was behind global warming (McGill 2009). David Keith, who holds the Canada Research Chair in Energy and the Environment at the University of Calgary told me, 'I have never heard an argument that the current rise in CO_2 is caused by temperature.'

There is, for the record, another camp that refutes the idea of any global warming at all. This group is often disparagingly referred to as 'deniers' and is currently the target of such vitriolic criticism and threats that I shall refrain from further comment – in the interests of my health.

Is the End of the World Nigh?

Let's suppose that anthropogenic climate change really is the mother of all threats. Is aviation as guilty as environmentalists would have us believe? Some of the answers are surprising. The United Nations Food and Agriculture Organisation issued a report in 2006 entitled *Livestock's Long Shadow* which stated that no less than 18 per cent of the world's CO_2 comes from cattle (Henderson 2007). If true, this would render damage by road and air transport insignificant by comparison. The idea behind this amazing report is that cows expel methane by way of (how can I put this delicately?) flatulence, and methane is around 22 times more potent than CO_2. Hence, in 'CO_2-equivalent' terms, the cows are guilty in the eyes of the United Nations. Animal rights groups rushed to capitalise on the study, urging that we should all become vegetarians. Michael O'Leary, characteristically, said that we should start shooting animals (O'Leary 2006). However, the UN's findings were hotly contested by the US Environmental Protection Agency, which retorted that livestock contributes a mere 2.4 per cent of total greenhouse emissions (Henderson 2007). Just in case the cows really are the culprits, the Japanese have a solution up their sleeves. Researchers at the Obihiro University of Agriculture and Veterinary Medicine have concocted a formula for a feed that can stave off flatulence and, consequently, counter global warming (Takahashi 2009). So, that's all right, then.

There is seemingly no end to the scare stories. Harvard University physicist Dr Alex Wissner-Gross wrote in *The Sunday Times* that the millions of us who spend hours every day simply browsing the Internet create a carbon footprint that adds up to an astounding 2 per cent of international emissions, actually equalling the global footprint of the aviation industry. The rationale for this extraordinary statement is that websites are far from being ephemeral in nature. Each website comprises files stored on a server somewhere, and that consumes electricity, the creation of which in turn consumes fossil fuels. Dr Wissner-Gross even suggested that the operating efficiency of some high-profile sites was remarkably poor, citing Her Majesty the Queen's site as being as low as 54 per cent and the BBC site at just 49 per cent. The reported research went on to suggest that spending several minutes using Google to perform a search can generate as much CO_2 as boiling a kettle (Leake and Woods 2009). Another idea that is frequently waved in front of concerned Internet surfers is that Google's white screen is more damaging to the environment owing to the additional energy needed. Incidentally, Google hotly contests such conclusions yet remains secretive concerning its carbon emissions, merely saying that it is committed to carbon neutrality (Google 2009). The Internet is, naturally, awash with endless anecdotes and invidious comparisons designed to create doubt, perpetuate guilt and stoke fear.

The litmus test is how public opinion has been affected by the contradictory theories offered up by scientists, politicians, interest groups and the media. In the United Kingdom *The Times* conducted a poll to estimate the percentage of the population prepared to accept scientific evidence in support of anthropogenic global warming. The result? Just 41 per cent. One reason offered as an explanation is that the recession is simply pushing climate change further down the agenda for many people (Riddell and Webster 2009). As illustrated by Figure 7.1, a similar survey in the United States revealed even more scepticism, with only 36 per cent of those polled believing that human activity is resulting in global warming – a reduction of 11 per cent compared to the previous year (Pew Research 2009). To put this in perspective, 37 per cent of Americans believe in haunted houses (Lyons 2005)!

Response to the question: 'Is there solid evidence the earth is warming?'

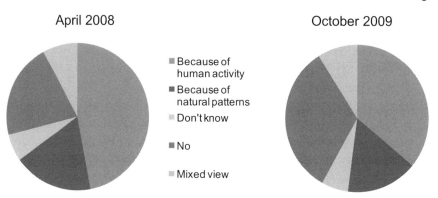

Figure 7.1   Global warming opinions, 2008 and 2009
Source: Pew Research Center for the People and the Press (2009).

How can mere mortals divine the truth? Perhaps we should turn to spiritual leaders to show us the right path.

God is Green

The impressively-named Evangelical Climate Change Initiative, comprising a group of 85 or so Christian leaders in the United States, captured some attention in 2006 at the National Press Club in Washington by declaring that damage sustained in God's world 'is an offence against God Himself' (Laumer 2006). Somehow, that particular campaign did not seem to get very far. However, one must look to the United Kingdom for more practical advice from the Church. Rowan Williams, the Archbishop of Canterbury, ruffled some feathers by likening moral choices over the environment with those over sex (Leake 2006). However, Richard Chartres, the Bishop of London and the third most senior bishop in the Church of England, went one better than his boss by making a clumsy but eminently newsworthy statement about moral choice. He said, 'Making selfish choices such as flying on holiday or buying a large car are a symptom of sin.' Ryanair's Michael O'Leary had the temerity to say what many were thinking. 'The Bishop of London has got empty churches – presumably if no one went on holiday perhaps they might turn up and listen to his sermons. God bless the bishop' (Clement 2006). Needless to say, the media lapped it up and the fall-out came to a head in a Channel 4 television documentary aired on 12 February 2007 entitled *God is Green*, in which a reporter is seen persuading the bishop to sign a pledge not to travel by air. Bishop Chartres henceforth gritted his teeth and endured some lengthy rail journeys to conferences in Germany and Romania, but his luck finally ran out when he had to attend an environmental meeting at an Arctic location only accessible by air (Bates 2007).

One cannot fault the bishop over his green credentials. After all, he has initiated steps such as an energy audit of the United Kingdom's draughtiest buildings – its churches and cathedrals. Even Lambeth Palace, the residence of Archbishop Rowan Williams, was censured for its use of inefficient light bulbs, rather than low-energy alternatives (Leake 2006).

The above example serves to illustrate the depth of emotion and ridiculousness that frequently surrounds the subject of environmental responsibility. However, in a world dominated by political correctness, there is no margin for error when it comes to such a highly-charged subject as the environment. But why is it that aviation attracts so much attention? Where did we go wrong?

Binge Flying

Well, one obvious source of criticism stems from one of the airline industry's biggest successes. The rampant low-cost carrier phenomenon of the last decade fuelled demand for air travel for the masses in much the same way that the charter airlines did almost 40 years earlier. The low-cost airlines democratised travel by air. The emergence of low fares spurred a revolution in short-haul travel where people often fly just for the sake of it. We have all heard and read anecdotes of how prospective travellers would seek out a flight not based upon a destination, but purely upon whether they could get a great deal. Travellers were simply exercising freedom in how they decided to spend their money. Seemingly overnight, everyone had become obsessed with the idea of spending almost every weekend cheerfully enduring airport queues and cramming themselves into – yes! – new, fuel-efficient aircraft at next-to-nothing fares. And who was going to stop them feeding their addiction?

Ironically, the term 'binge flying' was allegedly coined by Mark Ellingham, the man who founded the *Rough Guides*, a series of publications that revolutionised recreational travel and encouraged a whole generation of holidaymakers to seek and fly to far-off destinations. Ellingham has backtracked and now likens the destructive effects of binge flying as 'the new tobacco' (Hill 2007).

There is a familiar argument that unbridled tourism ultimately destroys the fabric of exotic and previously untouched destinations. Now we are being told that the journey itself is destroying the fabric of the planet. Is this a question of ethics? Should behaviour be regulated through the imposition of punitive taxes? What about freedom of choice in an enlightened and democratic society? These are questions for which there are no easy answers. However, one question that can be addressed is whether individual travel behaviour decisions are rational in the light of all the information thrown at us concerning the environment.

Guilty of the Charge of Destroying the Planet

No modern air traveller can honestly claim to be unaware of the environmental debate. We are bombarded with messages designed to invoke anything from a twinge of guilt right up to fear of censure for failing to take our environmental responsibilities seriously. Yet even the 'greenest' traveller is capable of making environmentally irrational decisions bordering on subliminal hypocrisy.

There is evidence to support this proposition. A study of over 1,000 people on attitudes to air travel, released by the UK Department for Transport in 2008, found that two-thirds of respondents agreed that flying damages the environment. However, just 1 per cent admitted that their concern extends as far as actually reducing their air travel. The cost of travel was deemed to have a much greater impact than environmental damage on decisions not to fly (Department for Transport 2008).

Similarly, two British universities, Loughborough and Exeter, conducted research into the public attitude to aviation and the environment and found broadly similar attitudes. Loughborough's Propensity to Fly study found that 88 per cent of respondents were willing or very willing to reduce energy use in the home. However, when asked whether they would not fly within the next 12 months, the percentage dropped to just 26 per cent. Exeter University concluded from its research that the worst offenders are the 'green-living idealists' who heavily promote recycling and energy efficiency in the home (Vaughan 2009). Its study revealed that some respondents even believed that they deserved to fly as a reward for their green efforts. One individual reported, 'I recycle 100% of what I can, so that makes me feel less guilty about flying as much as I do' (Adam 2008). As expected, Ryanair's CEO, Michael O'Leary, is more forthright, accusing 'hairy environmentalists' of being hypocrites for eating organic food flown into Britain. 'Why don't they eat British turnips all winter if they want to save flights?' he asked (Webster 2007).

What this shows is that there is a long way to go before we can expect to see a modification of perception, attitude and rational judgement. A good defence for such inconsistency from travellers is that the whole subject of the extent to which aviation actually damages the environment is shrouded in confusion.

But are some of us guiltier than others?

The Top Polluting Nations

Conventional belief is that the guiltiest nations are the most industrialised and highly developed and that these nations should shoulder the responsibility for doing something about the environmental damage. Conventional wisdom suggests that the United States is the biggest culprit. However, a leading source of global risk intelligence, Maplecroft, has suggested that the top five offenders are Australia, the United States, Canada, the Netherlands and Saudi Arabia. This startling conclusion is based on a composite of three indicators including total CO_2 emissions from energy, CO_2 emissions from energy use per capita and cumulative CO_2 emissions from energy use (Maplecroft 2009). If we limit the comparison to just one of these three components – that of CO_2 emissions from fuel combustion per capita – then the top five is even more bizarre, the offenders being Qatar, the United Arab Emirates, Bahrain, Kuwait and the Netherlands Antilles (IEA Statistics 2009). The State of Qatar, to its credit, is working hard to develop a gas-to-liquid solution to replace aviation kerosene, as we shall see later in this chapter.

The Kyoto Protocol came into force in 2005 with the objective of stabilising and reconstructing greenhouse gas concentrations in the atmosphere in order to prevent dangerous anthropogenic interference with the climate system. The accords set legally binding targets for the reduction of greenhouse gas emissions, amounting to an average reduction of 5.2 per cent from 1990 levels by 2012. The accords were ratified by 184 parties of the United Nations Climate Convention, with the stunning exception of the largest polluting nation at the time, the United States. Environmentalists blame former US President George W. Bush for spurning the Kyoto Protocol on the basis that the provisions would be too costly to implement and potentially damage US interests. Former Vice President Al Gore famously accused Bush of a 'stunning display of moral cowardice'.

The United Nations climate conference in Copenhagen in December 2009 failed to elicit a new climate treaty to map out a reduction of greenhouse gases by the industrialised nations. This was largely due to the arrogance of many of the developed nations and their failure to pay enough attention to the needs of developing nations, although it must be acknowledged that the summit did succeed in focusing minds on the issues. The magnitude of this challenge can be appreciated by reference to cartograms, where territories are deliberately distorted and resized to reveal information about a particular variable. The values of the variable are substituted for land area. Figure 7.2 shows the distribution of global population, and Figure 7.3 illustrates a redistribution of land mass according to greenhouse gas emissions. Unsurprisingly, the industrialised nations' share of responsibility, as measured by population, exceeds that of

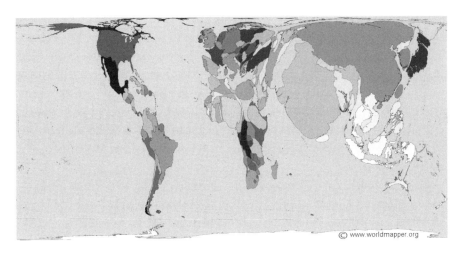

Shows the relative proportion of population of each territory

Figure 7.2   Cartogram of world population

Source: Worldmapper. © Copyright SASI Group (University of Sheffield).

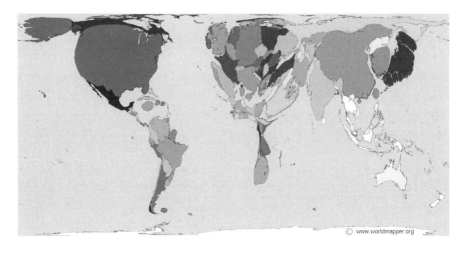

Shows the relative proportion of all greenhouse gas emissions
emanating from each territory

Figure 7.3   Cartogram of greenhouse gas emissions
Source: Worldmapper. © Copyright SASI Group (University of Sheffield).

developing nations. Africa, in particular, stands out as a continent
with relatively little responsibility for greenhouse gas generation,
yet obviously registers significantly in terms of human existence.
Equally striking is the weighting of emissions responsibility
towards the United States.

The Copenhagen climate conference of December 2009 also
failed to resolve the question of whether major developing
nations such as China and India are willing to place limits on the
growth of their own emissions (Von Bűlow 2009). China overtook
the United States as the biggest CO_2 emitter in 2008 although,
on a per capita basis, the United States still outstrips China by a
factor of four.

To place things in perspective, consider this. In 2006 China's
incremental CO_2 emissions were exactly equivalent to the *total*
CO_2 emissions of the United Kingdom (IEA Statistics 2009).
It seems safe to assume, therefore, that China holds the key to
bringing about a realistic impact in controlling global emissions.
Yet Richard Dyer, transport and climate change campaigner for
Friends of the Earth, completely disagrees: 'The West is mainly
responsible for the problem of climate change by pumping most

of the carbon into the atmosphere in the first place. So the onus is on the West to take the lead and set an example.' That's a fair point and who are we to deny developing nations the opportunity to develop? The fact remains that, compared to the dizzying pace of China's industrial charge, switching to economy light bulbs in Lambeth Palace is not going to make one ha'penny of difference to the fate of planet earth.

Where Does Aviation Fit into the Picture?

Over the last few years environmentalists have been sharpening their knives and scouring around for the guilty. It is hardly surprising that accusing fingers are pointing at aviation.

It is worth pointing out at this stage that the effect of aviation on the environment extends beyond the emission of CO_2. Airports are a perennial source of concern because noise emissions affect the quality of life of those living in their vicinity, to say nothing of the impact of land take, water pollution, waste management and so on. If we go back just one generation we would find that concerns over airport expansion mostly centred on noise. Today, the economic and social issues concerning airports revolve around carbon emissions. For example, the case for a third runway at London's Heathrow airport is built on a calculation that considers benefit to the overall economy, the cost of construction and, crucially, a 'shadow' cost of additional CO_2 produced. The economic case for airport development must be evaluated decades into the future and, unsurprisingly, it is quite impossible to accurately predict the cost of CO_2. Consequently, the issue became highly charged by politics and emotion and, at the time of writing, the new Conservative–Liberal Democrat government has been swayed by such arguments, as well as by the costs involved, and has not only cancelled the whole project, but also ruled out runway expansion at Stansted and Gatwick.

Such issues have not deterred rapidly developing economies in Asia from pressing ahead with airport development. China's 11th Five Year Plan calls for 49 new airports to be built between 2006 and 2010, at an investment of $18 billion. In the longer term, an amazing 97 new airports are planned between 2007 and 2020 (ImpactLab 2008). I confidently suggest that the arguments supporting development on such a massive scale were minimally influenced by an assessment of CO_2 emissions.

The current focus on aviation's contribution to environmental damage is pollution from aircraft. Principal aircraft emissions are carbon dioxide, water vapour and the combination of nitric oxide and nitrogen dioxide, which together are termed NO_x. Finally, aircraft emit sulphur oxides and soot. For many years the principal villain was thought to be NO_x, as it affects ozone chemistry. Ozone is well known for shielding the earth's surface from damaging ultraviolet radiation, but it is also a greenhouse gas and increases in response to the presence of NO_x.

However, as we have already seen, the current flavour of the environmental debate, and therefore the one that really matters, is the amount of CO_2 generated. The amount of CO_2 produced by aircraft engines is directly related to fuel consumption. Chemistry dictates that for every unit of fuel burnt, 3.15 units of CO_2 are produced. A reasonable benchmark is that aircraft contribute approximately 2 per cent of global carbon emissions. The IPCC believes that aviation is responsible for about 3.5 per cent of overall anthropogenic climate change. Aviation accounts for roughly 13 per cent of CO_2 emissions from all transportation sources (IPCC 2009). This puts aviation roughly on a par with emissions in the information, communication and technology sector (see Figure 7.4).

A value of 2 per cent seems almost paltry but, as we shall see in a moment, it assumes a somewhat different significance when the rapid growth of the industry is taken into account. It cannot be denied that the air transport industry has made huge strides in improving its operating efficiency alongside its explosive growth. For example, civil aviation now contributes 8 per cent of world gross domestic product (GDP), and its airlines convey more than 2.2 billion people per year. Around 40 per cent of international tourists travel by air. Airfreight carries 40 per cent (by value) of interregional export goods. Since 1970 the industry has doubled in size every 15 years. And this, of course, is the problem. The airline industry's trade association, IATA, is fond of debunking 'persistent myths' by stressing that airline fuel efficiency has improved by 20 per cent in the past decade. This is certainly true, but it is an inescapable fact that global

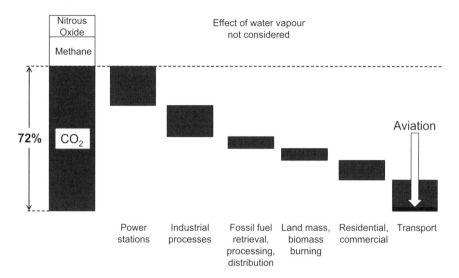

Figure 7.4   Greenhouse gases – aviation's share
Source: Derived from IPCC statistics

CO_2 emissions have been inexorably rising. For example, climate researchers for the Omega group of universities that provide impartial advice to the industry have pointed out that aviation carbon emissions have grown by 42 per cent between 1990 and 2005 (Raper 2009). The Council of the European Aerospace Societies separately confirmed the calculation by reporting that CO_2 emissions grew globally by 2–3 percent per year from 1990 to 2004 (CEAS 2009). The UK government's Office of National Statistics says that carbon emissions from aviation more than trebled between 1980 and 2006 (Department of Transport 2009). None of this is surprising, but the industry prefers not to talk about it. A more honest approach would be to focus on the dramatic improvements in unit efficiencies which are, it has to be admitted, admirable.

The most vital statistic is the one predicted for the middle of this century. The dilemma is how to appease aviation's critics and the activists while ensuring that air transport's contribution to society and global well-being is not jeopardised. The Intergovernmental Panel on Climate Change has produced scenarios in which the range of CO_2 aircraft emissions expected in 2050 swings wildly from 1.6 times the 1992 value to a whopping ten times the 1992 value (IPCC 2007).

So far in this chapter we have seen that the aviation industry is faced with a series of seemingly insurmountable dilemmas concerning the environment. First, the attitude of the individual to environmental issues is often irrational and unpredictable. Second, there is no clear-cut, simple and universal agreement on whether the planet is actually being damaged or not. Third, the world has come to depend on air transport for both global economic function and social needs, so any reduction in air transport appears unthinkable as well as unworkable. Fourth, long-term forecasts of aviation carbon emissions vary dramatically. What should be done, and by whom?

The aviation industry has been far from idle and has been anxious to announce self-imposed targets to control future emissions. The manufacturers, airports, air traffic service providers and airlines are all putting their weight behind a common goal to achieve a 1.5 per cent annual fuel efficiency improvement until 2020, with carbon-neutral growth from then on. The target also includes a halving of carbon emissions in 2050 compared to 2005 levels. British Airways Chief Executive Willie Walsh presented the numbers, on behalf of IATA, at a United Nations leadership forum on climate change in New York in September 2009. Greenpeace was predictably unimpressed, calling the measures 'an elaborate conjuring trick' and a 'complete greenwash' (Greenpeace 2009). Richard Dyer, transport and climate change campaigner of Friends of the Earth, believes that the 1.5 per cent annual improvement is really just 'business as usual', as the industry has been achieving that rate of improvement for a number of years.

However, ICAO held a 'High Level Meeting' on international aviation and climate change in Montreal in October 2009 and thrashed out a separate set of targets. Delegates recommended that the industry should strive for a 2 per cent annual fuel efficiency improvement, rather than the 1.5 per cent proposed by the airlines themselves. ICAO also supplanted IATA's emission reduction targets, preferring to steer the industry towards an 'aspirational' goal of a further average annual 2 per cent fuel efficiency improvement from 2021 to 2050 (ICAO 2009). Although the ICAO declaration talks in vague terms about 'economic measures', the airlines would have preferred to see a commitment to put clear market measures in place. This is a point of view expressed by Chris Schroeder, Head of Corporate Social Responsibility, Environment and Fuel Optimisation at Qatar Airways. His airline is a member of the Airline Global Deal group which comprises leading international airlines as well as an international NGO called The Climate Group. 'There is a clear danger that the least developed countries might push for a levy that doesn't take fuel efficiency into account. It could cost the industry billions with no return through environmental projects', he says.

Qatar Airways is a perfect example of an airline that has taken its environmental responsibilities seriously. The airline operates a fuel-efficient fleet of aircraft with an average age of just 3.2 years, and has a clear environmental strategy in place, embracing elements such as fuel management, environmental management systems and communications. Says Schroeder, 'We have positioned ourselves at the forefront to protect ourselves politically, distinguish ourselves from the competition, as well as influence the perception of the travelling public'. The new 'Ministry of Environment' in Qatar intends to use Qatar Airways as a flagship for the country and to set an example for others to follow.

Aircraft Design and Air Traffic Management Measures

Efforts and progress being made to address the environmental challenge have been commendably pre-emptive, rather than reactive. The aircraft and engine manufacturers in particular have devoted huge resources to improving airframe efficiency, fuel burn, maintainability, plus the development of a steady stream of innovations designed to make their products more attractive. Naturally, the original equipment manufacturers have been spurred on by competitive pressure and it is a happy consequence that their efforts have also paid off by making aircraft cleaner and quieter. Philippe Fonta is Head of Environmental Policy at Airbus and explains that the approach is to consider the entire life-cycle of the aircraft: 'Our responsibility is from the design, to the manufacturing including the supply chain, then the transportation of parts from one site to another and to the final assembly line, and helping airlines in their operations. We have also developed some environmentally-friendly practices for recycling aircraft.' All the major airframe and engine manufacturers have put in place an environmental management system based on the internationally recognised ISO 14001 standard.

However, it takes more than aircraft design to reduce the impact of carbon emissions. Airspace optimisation is an area where much opportunity lies. Industry representation organisations, such as IATA, have fostered and encouraged the debate. Local initiatives, such as the Asia and South Pacific Initiative to Reduce Emissions (ASPIRE), have accelerated the introduction of more efficient operating procedures and airway routings. Continuous Descent Approach, also known as Optimised Descent Profile, is becoming more prevalent in Europe as well as in the United States where typical savings of around 450 kilogrammes per landing are feasible (Associated Press 2009). Overall potential fuel-burn savings as a result of all improvements in air traffic management and operational procedures could amount to anything between 8 and 18 per cent (IPCC 2009).

Airspace optimisation techniques can be introduced within the scope of relatively modest applications of new technologies. However, in order for aviation to be liberated from the shackles of total reliance on the availability of fossil fuels, a monumental leap forward is required. But there have been some extraordinary own goals.

Designing for the Environment is Not so Easy

Throughout history, whenever the need for innovation has grown strong enough, human endeavour has been duly rewarded. The Darwinian principle of survival of the fittest will never fail, given sufficient determination and persistence. Yet not all dramatic technical breakthroughs in aviation have had happy endings. The chequered career of Concorde illustrates the difficulties of reconciling a technological breakthrough with hard economics.

It is sometimes puzzling how the quest for an environmentally acceptable solution can be blinded to obvious operational, economic and market impacts. The UK Greener by Design group once put forward a serious proposal to study the development of an aircraft design that would have an operational range of no more than 7,500 kilometres, on the basis that this distance is optimum in terms of payload fuel efficiency (Greener by Design 2001). This extraordinary idea of transforming long-distance air travel to a greater number of multi-sector journeys conveniently glossed over the implications of changing the entire structure of long-haul airline networks.

The fabled Sonic Cruiser proposal, unveiled by Boeing in 2001, could have been an embarrassing environmental own goal. In a stark attempt to steal some of the limelight from the recently launched A380, Boeing dusted off one of a series of new aircraft designs it had been developing. It was a stunning design for a transonic aircraft that promised to reduce transatlantic journey times by as much as 75 minutes, capable of flying just shy of the speed of sound at altitudes of over 40,000 feet. The Sonic Cruiser had all the makings of a marketing triumph, with twin vertical tails and forward canard design. Airline executives salivated over the sleek, brushed aluminium models that Boeing salesmen reverently placed on boardroom tables. Continental Airlines described the aircraft as being the best home run that Boeing had ever hit. American Airlines wanted to secure the entire early production in order to lock out competitors (Wallace 2002). Singapore Airlines, Emirates and Virgin Atlantic were all gushing enthusiastically about the aircraft. Indeed, for a while it seemed as though the future of commercial aviation lay in fleets of medium-sized Sonic Cruisers, shrinking journey times and heralding a major shift in aircraft technology. However, reality quickly struck home when it transpired that travellers' appetite for shorter journey times was not as keen as their appetite for lower fares, and pricing for riding a Sonic Cruiser would almost certainly have been at a premium. Critically, the operating costs of the aircraft would have offered no appreciable advantage over subsonic alternatives so, in the face of mounting doubts, the onset of the recession and the aftermath of the 11 September 2001 terrorist attacks, the project was abandoned in 2002. Boeing sensibly redirected its attention to developing what was to become the 787, a less revolutionary but far more appropriate solution.

What is fascinating about the Sonic Cruiser story is that fuel efficiency was never a big issue. We shall probably never know, but it was likely that the Sonic Cruiser would have consumed *more* fuel than other contemporary aircraft. It symbolised the swan song of an era in which fabulous technical achievements in aviation were driven mostly by style. From now on, technical achievement in the skies is strictly focused on a blend of practicality, economics and due concern for the environment – and not necessarily in that order.

Some visionaries believe that nuclear propulsion is the key to breaking the link between aviation and fossil fuels. The Soviet Union and the United States seriously considered military applications of nuclear power in the 1950s and the United States even flight-tested an onboard nuclear reactor. The attraction of nuclear power is that CO_2 emissions would be eliminated and refuelling would become a thing of the past. The UK government-funded Omega project has called for research into new concepts, suggesting that nuclear-powered aircraft are a solution beyond 2050 (Times Online 2008). Yes, really. But we do not need to wait until 2050 for zero-emissions flying. That accolade already belongs to the German-inspired Antares DLR-H2 which made a landmark CO_2-free test flight in July 2009 using fuel cells (Turner 2009). Zero emissions is closer than you might think, as the private aviation company NetJets aims to be completely carbon-neutral by 2012, due to a mandatory carbon offsetting programme (Aviation and the Environment 2009).

Mainstream air transport will not achieve anything like carbon-neutral flying in the immediate future, but serious moves are afoot to reduce dependence on jet fuel.

Alternative Fuels – The Holy Grail

This is a hot subject, so let's start by putting things in perspective. Planet earth consumes over 30 billion barrels of oil per annum, or around 100 million barrels per day. The global population is estimated to grow from 6.7 billion today to 9.1 billion by the middle of the century. Clearly, replacing fossil fuels with any form of biological process will be a huge challenge, particularly for aviation, where dependence on fossil fuel is especially critical. Also, it is simply impossible to envisage a long-term solution that competes with the production of food. The United Nations food agency believes that food production will need to increase by 70 per cent over the next 40 years if we are to avoid large-scale famine (BBC News 2009). The great fear is that the growing demand for biofuels as a replacement for fossil fuels could jeopardise our ability to feed ourselves. First-generation biofuels comprise fuels derived from sources such as starch, sugar, animal fats and vegetable oil. Clearly, such sources could be a threat to food supplies, but the ethical arguments have been aired and it is widely accepted that the food versus fuel argument is legitimate. Biologist and genetic pioneer Craig Venter has stated, 'Corn to ethanol is just a bad experiment' (Venter 2008). Philippe Fonta, Head of Sustainable Development at Airbus, stresses, 'Obviously, we do not want to enter into competition with the food chain, so we are experimenting with second- or third-generation biofuels, for instance, made out of algae.'

Second-generation biofuel focuses on the residual components of food crops, such as stems, husks and leaves, as well as industry waste such as wood chips and pulp from fruit-pressing. In this category we may also find specific crops such as jatropha and switch grass. Third-generation biofuel comes from the growth of algae. Numerous questions have been raised about algae as a potential replacement for oil, such as energy content, water supply for growth, land use and potential carbon emissions. However, of all the alternatives, opinion does seem to be weighted in favour of algae, and the concept has attracted significant capital. For example, US$600 million has been invested by Exxon Mobil in what will become the biggest biofuel development project to date (Gelsi 2009).

Conventional aviation fuel is a hard act to follow. It has high energy content, does not freeze at high altitudes and is stable across a wide range of operating temperatures. As aviation is very much a global business, it is not possible to change the type of fuel used in one part of the world without changing it in another at the same time. Aircraft depend on compatible infrastructure and systems, so an overnight technological shift is simply not possible. Says Philippe Fonta, 'That's why we are orienting the research to what we call "drop-in" fuels that have comparable characteristics to conventional fuel and can be used as a blend.'

Currently, a huge range of blended solutions is under development and there have been some impressive tests, as airlines and manufacturers rush to demonstrate their green credentials. Virgin Atlantic has plumped for isobutanol as an alternative fuel, with Sir Richard Branson praising the solution as 'wonderful' (*Aviation News* 2009). Qatar Airways achieved a world 'first' by conducting a revenue-earning flight from London Gatwick to Doha with an A340-600 powered by a 50/50 mix of normal jet fuel and gas-to-liquid (GTL) kerosene in October 2009. The airline plans to adopt a 50 per cent blend of GTL kerosene for all flights from its Doha base by 2012 and Shell, along with Qatar Petroleum, is constructing a plant with the aim of 1 million tonnes of GTL production by the same year. Qatar Airways' Chris Schroeder says, 'We're not saying that GTL is the silver bullet, but it is definitely a significant milestone and gives us some independence from fluctuating oil prices.' KLM followed hot on the heels of Qatar Airways with its own GTL-powered flight in November 2009.

However, not all experiments have gone according to plan. In 2008 jatropha, a bush widely cultivated in India and Malaysia, was being hailed as a biofuel panacea, as it was found that the crushed seeds yield oil that can be used to power almost any engine. Jatropha is not, however, as friendly as it sounds. Just four seeds from the highly toxic fruit of the plant could prove fatal, yet it has been successfully harnessed to combat fever, malaria and constipation. BP announced a £32 million investment in a joint venture with a British biofuel company called D1 Oils to drive the development. Interest extended to other parts of the world, with Air New Zealand successfully conducting a test flight of a 747-400 with a 50/50 jatropha blend and Continental Airlines also testing a 737-800 with a jatropha and algae blend. One year later, however, BP abandoned the project, having discovered that the agricultural conditions needed to produce sufficient quantities of the crop would interfere with food production (Mackenzie 2009).

A UK think tank, Policy Exchange, has suggested that if 80 per cent of jet fuel could be derived from, or blended with, biofuels by mid-century, then European aviation greenhouse gas emissions could be reduced by 60 per cent (Caldecott 2009). Airbus's Fonta says, 'Alternative fuels can play a substantial role and up to 25 per cent use of alternative fuels could be reached in 2025 for the sector.'

If that sounds ambitious, then consider the vision of Craig Venter, the man whose credentials include the sequencing of the human genome. He believes that the only way biology can make a true impact on replacing fossil fuel as an energy source, and without interfering with the cost of food or its production, is to actually use CO_2 itself as a feedstock. This so-called fourth-generation fuel is under development and could make a debut within a couple of years (Zakaria 2008).

Not everyone is so optimistic when it comes to development times for new fuel sources. A leading expert in biomass energy, Professor Claus Felby, is convinced that first-generation biofuels will be around for several decades, implying that competition between agriculture and biofuels will intensify. Something has got to give. There is a limit to the degree to which pesticides and fertilisers can improve agricultural yields, and there are significant moral, social and political hurdles to overcome. It seems likely that the only way to completely decouple food production and energy is to rely on algae and, beyond that, fourth-generation biofuels. Felby believes that it will 20 years before sufficient quantities of biofuels become available (Murray 2009). In the meantime, aviation's best hope seems to be pinned on saltwater plants known as halophytes. Boeing, Honeywell and the Masdar Institute of Science and Technology in Abu Dhabi are researching how jet fuel can be extracted from halophytes without disrupting food production (RenewableEnergyWorld 2009).

The Greening of the Fleets

Aviation cannot afford to wait until biofuels become readily available. Technical improvements to both airframe and engine are coming thick and fast and have a major role to play until the fuel challenge is overcome. Whereas design improvements used to be driven principally by competitive pressures between the manufacturers, the imperative to innovate simply to get the deal has been augmented by a need to appease the growing army of environmentalists. Indeed, the original equipment manufacturers have never been so motivated to design their new products with the environment in mind. Not only do you have to *be* green, but you have to be *seen* to be green.

Pressure on manufacturers to green up the world's aircraft fleet has come from all sources. The airlines themselves are not averse to coming up with some surprising initiatives to spur on the manufacturers, which naturally serve their own ends as well. One of the most interesting of these was promoted by easyJet, the British low-cost carrier. Their ecoJet is a conceptual design unveiled in 2007 to show the world that easyJet is deadly serious about the environment. The airline produced a model of its design, rather as Boeing had done for the abortive Sonic Cruiser, but with a completely different objective in mind. Instead of a sleek gas-guzzler, the ecoJet would have forward-direction swept wings to minimise drag while maintaining laminar flow, rear-mounted open rotor engines integrated into a double tailplane, and the airframe would be constructed of light materials. Former Chief Executive Officer Andrew Harrison said, 'This is not *Star Trek*; this is within our grasp' (Moores 2007). EasyJet suggested that its design would be 25 per cent quieter than similar aircraft, such as the A320 or 737, would be 50 per cent more fuel-efficient, and would produce 50 per cent less CO_2 and 75 per cent less NO_x. If that is not already enough, the composite airframe would contribute yet another 15 per cent in efficiency and, yes, yet another 10 per cent gain in fuel reduction and CO_2 could be expected from the use of avionics linked with future air traffic management systems. The ecoJet could be delivered in 2015, according to easyJet.

It's easy to scoff at the ecoJet's futuristic design as being exactly what Andrew Harrison said it was not – something out of *Star Trek*. However, supporters of the ecoJet can argue that if the advance of technology continues at its historical pace, many of the seemingly ambitious targets could be within the grasp of the manufacturers.

Two obstacles stand in the way.

First, it is by no means certain that technological advances will result in an exact extrapolation of the past. Perhaps we have not reached the plateau, but future incremental benefits are likely to get smaller, and the investment needed to achieve them correspondingly larger. This will not stop engine manufacturers racing to stay ahead of the curve. All the major suppliers, Rolls-Royce, CFM International, General Electric and Pratt & Whitney have plans to produce advanced turbofans in the middle of the next decade and all are promising efficiency improvements in the order of 15 per cent. Open rotor technology, with fan blades turning outside the casing of the engine, seems to be the direction in which most are moving. If an improvement of 15 per cent in efficiency could be achieved in the next round of engine technology, then extrapolating the same rate of improvement would indeed result in a doubling of fuel efficiency in the 2030s, although this would be somewhat later than the ecoJet target of 2015. The improvement curve is getting flatter, and any engine development must be ultimately constrained by a need for some kind of fuel. Thin air has already been harnessed for thrust generation by increasing the bypass ratio of turbofans, but we are not talking about gliders here.

Airbus gave a cautious welcome to the ecoJet, conscious of the golden rule that says 'never criticise a customer'. And this brings us to the second obstacle standing in the way of the ecoJet's success. As we saw in Chapter 2, Airbus and Boeing are enjoying considerable success with their single-aisle products and do not believe that the technology benefits are good enough for them to replace these with completely new models in the short term, despite the probability of geared turbofans becoming available well before the end of the economic life-cycle of the A320 and 737 aircraft. All-new aircraft models in this size category may not become a reality until the 2020s as derivative technologies are currently more attractive and can be developed with less cost and less risk. If this turns out to be the case, then the manufacturers will have postponed, although not squandered, an opportunity to bring a completely new technology package to the market.

Richard Dyer believes that it is a mistake to commit to large infrastructure projects, especially airports, at a time when it is unclear whether the technology really will develop as hoped. 'Some of the aspirational goals for the future are potentially quite shaky,' he says, because their achievement may depend on financial and market considerations. 'It's very difficult for governments to allow for runway development and then say later, "You can't use them because you didn't deliver the technology that you promised".'

The Market Mechanism Minefield

Airbus's Head of Sustainable Development, Philippe Fonta, believes that the industry's self-imposed targets, namely an annual 1.5 per cent fuel efficiency improvement, carbon-neutral growth from 2020 and a halving of carbon emissions in 2050 compared to the 2005 level, are certainly within our grasp through a combination of measures: 'It will be achieved by technology. It will be achieved by the introduction of alternative fuels. It will be achieved by implementing fair and equitable market-based mechanisms at a worldwide level in order to get additional credit for reductions we cannot achieve simply through technology.'

There may be global agreement on the levels of environmental targets, but how to get there is a very different matter. Technology has a big role to play, together with the various initiatives to find a new propulsion fuel. The real controversy lies in the market mechanism minefield where parochialism of local interests battles against the pragmatism of a global solution. The International Civil Aviation Organisation (ICAO) has pushed for the logic of a global approach, but this has not stopped the Europeans forging ahead with a plan to include international aviation within its own Emission Trading Scheme (EU ETS) from 2012. An Emission Trading Scheme, incidentally, allows the trading of emissions permits between countries and sometimes businesses as part of a 'cap and trade' approach to limiting emissions. On the face of it, this seems like a pragmatic way of managing a complex issue. Operators of installations that create emissions receive allowances, conferring the right to emit a certain amount of CO_2 each year. These allowances may be traded in the most cost-effective manner for the operator. Thus, if an operator needs to exceed the cap, then additional allowances may be purchased. Alternatively, unused emissions can be banked to cover for future emissions, or else sold. Whether an operator does actually purchase emissions or invests in better technology is purely an economic decision. However, this is not the panacea it seems.

One problem is that the true value of emissions trading will depend entirely on which year is selected as the 'cap'. Capping air transport at 2008 levels is estimated to generate around 17 per cent less CO_2 emissions in 2012, for example (European Union

2005). However, the European Commission has dragged its feet over the issue. The original idea was to base the cap on a three-year average of emissions between 2004 and 2006, but there are questions hanging over the accuracy of data and whether or not ground-based emissions should be included. In true European style a postponement is inevitable, which simply serves to compound the issue as, without any knowledge of the cap, airlines will find it more difficult to estimate their future need for allowances.

Another problem is that a significant number of aviation enterprises are far from prepared to enter the EU ETS in any case. A Norton Rose Group survey in mid-2009 indicated that a mere 6 per cent of businesses are fully prepared and one-third had failed to take any steps to prepare (Aviation Industry Group 2009).

Then, naturally, there is the vexed issue of the cost of the EU ETS scheme. One consultancy group has announced that the total cost of the scheme would exceed €1 billion (Point Carbon 2009). The CEO of British Airways, Willie Walsh, although supportive of the concept of emissions trading, has been vocal in his criticism of the EU's proposals scheme, arguing that the financial damage would exacerbate airline woes at the very time that the industry is on its knees (Domain-b.com 2008). Critics argue that the scheme would see fare rises and make European airlines less competitive. Even the legality of the European Commission's proposals has been questioned by the US Air Transport Association.

Emissions trading is not, of course, the only way to deal with the problem. Governments understandably harbour a strong desire to tax aviation fuel, rather than interfere with an individual's freedom to fly. After all, this would hardly be a vote-catching strategy. Yet taxing aviation fuel would in fact go some way towards controlling the seemingly uncontrollable phenomenon of binge flying: people will only curb their flying when it begins to hurt their pockets. Yet, however attractive a tax would be to governments and environmentalists, the reality is that it would be virtually impossible to introduce an equitable and sufficiently widespread scheme that would be effective. Furthermore, the airlines themselves are understandably vehemently opposed to any new taxes, especially at a time when they are struggling for their survival. Willie Walsh unsurprisingly dismisses taxation as no more than a 'blunt instrument' and argues that the value of the air passenger duty alone would be equivalent to offsetting the carbon emissions of the entire British Airways fleet twice over, pointing out, in addition, that none of the air passenger duty is used to support environmental projects (Walsh 2008). Friends of the Earth, on the other hand, is unapologetic when it comes to taxes on airlines. 'The industry has got away very lightly for decades,' says Richard Dyer.

Appealing to the conscience of the environmentally savvy traveller by selling carbon offsets is another part of the jigsaw. The idea is that passengers can voluntarily invest in carbon-reduction projects to balance the emissions that they generate by flying. One can argue that this is not really solving anything and is simply a mechanism to transfer the emissions responsibility elsewhere, in a sort of carbon carousel. Only a few dozen airline schemes are in existence, using a variety of methodologies and criteria. The International Air Transport Association has launched a standard offset programme based on an ICAO methodology, but take-up is unsurprisingly slow. Richard Dyer of Friends of the Earth is highly sceptical, saying, 'It's an excuse to carry on usual behaviour because you've done your bit.' One UK-based travel agency has gone further, saying that offsetting is a concept akin to a medieval pardon. Responsible Travel was one of the first travel agencies to introduce carbon offsetting in 2002 and became one of the first to discontinue the practice, arguing that the offset industry was unregulated and simply distracts tourists from a need to act responsibly (Reuters 2009).

All this only proves that it is one thing to shout about the environment, but it is quite another to put one's hand in one's pocket and stump up the money. Frankly, carbon offsetting is doomed to appeal to those wealthy enough, or guilty enough, to sign cheques so that others can be 'green' on their behalf.

In Conclusion

The whole question of the environment and the damage wrought upon it by human activity comes down to two rather straightforward, yet sharply opposing, propositions. First, we have the doomsday argument of the calamity howlers, which postulates that planet earth is being irreparably damaged by the selfish needs and desires of its inhabitants and that, if nothing is done to arrest the abuse we are wreaking on our home turf, we shall accelerate our own demise. Second, we have the envirosceptics, who refute human-induced global warming as a fraudulent myth constructed on pseudo-science in order to bamboozle a gullible public and perpetuate a massive new industry built to support it. Needless to say, each side pours scorn and contempt on the other.

Aviation finds itself inconveniently occupying a 'no man's land' between each side of the debate. Somehow the deadlock must be broken, yet it is preposterous to believe that we can accurately lay down the foundations for the shape of aviation 100 years from now. After all, the Victorians, arrogant as they were, would never have been so presumptuous as to try to accurately predict our current problems and then concoct answers to solve them. The best hope for aviation is to engage equally with both the calamity howlers and the envirosceptics, stop being so defensive, and work rapidly to build a globally united front. Aviation has no alternative but to adopt the precautionary principle and assume a responsibility for controlling carbon emissions. It is simply politically expedient to do so. The greater the effort to address the concerns of the environmentalists, the easier it will be to head off the stigma of a label which might read 'enviroheretic'.

Meanwhile, the various sides of the debate are destined to remain locked in combat. The economist Lord Nicolas Stern, who in 2007 authored an influential report on climate change to the UK Treasury at the Prime Minister's request, has labelled global warming deniers as 'flat-earthers' (Hundal 2009). Conversely, Professor Robert Essenhigh of Ohio State University says, 'Supporters of anthroprogenic climate change have too much politics and emotion embedded in them. They are the latest members of the Flat Earth Society and it would cost them too much in personal terms to step back and say, "I was wrong".'

Take your pick.

References

Adam, D., 2008. 'Green Idealists Fail to Make Grade, Says Study'. *Guardian*, 24 September. Also available at: http://www.guardian.co.uk/ environment/2008/sep/24/ethicalliving.recycling (accessed 25 May 2010).

Associated Press, 2009. 'New Plan to Reduce Planes' CO2 Emissions'. 31 March. Available at: http://www.physorg.com/news157702401.html (accessed 31 March 2009).

Aviation and the Environment, 2009. 'NetJets Europe Aims to be 100 Per Cent Carbon Neutral by 2012'. 10 November. Available at: http:// ubmaviationnews.com/newsArchhive/tabid/375/selectedmoduleid/822/ Articleid/3152/ren/r/Default.aspx (accessed 13 November 2009).

Aviation Industry Group, 2009. 'Only Six Percent are Fully Prepared for EU ETS'. 18 September. Available at: http://www.ubmaviationnews.com/ aig/news/newsarchive/tabid/375/selectedmoduleid/822/articleid/2581/ reftab/117/Default.aspx (accessed 20 November 2009).

Aviation News, 2009. 'TUI Travel Issues Environmental Results'. 13 August. Available at: http://www.ubmaviationnews.com/aig/News/ NewsArchive/tabid/375/selectedmoduleid/822/ArticleID/2144/Default. aspx (accessed 13 August 2009).

Bates. S., 2007. 'Environmentally Aware Bishop Pledges Not to Fly for a Year'. *Guardian*, 8 February. Also available at: http://www.guardian. co.uk/environment/2007/feb/08/religion.climatechange (accessed 26 May 2010).

BBC News, 2009. 'Food Production "Must Rise 70%"'. 12 October. Available at: http://news.bbc.co.uk/2/hi/europe/8303434.stm (accessed 12 October 2009).

Caldecott, B., 2009. 'Green Skies Thinking: Promoting the Development and Commercialisation of Sustainable Bio-jet Fuels'. 22 July. Available at: http://policyexchange.org.uk/publications/publication.cgi?id=129 (accessed 22 July 2009).

Calder, N., 1974. *The Weather Machine*. New York: Viking Press.

Clement, B., 2006. 'Ryanair Boss Attacks Bishop over Sermon on Sins of Low-fare Air Travel'. 27 July. Available at: http://www.independent. co.uk/news/business/news/ryanair-boss-attacks-bishop-over-sermaon-on-sins-of-lowfare-air-travel-409451.html (accessed 10 October 2009).

Council of European Aerospace Societies (CEAS), 2009. 'Towards Climate-optimized Aviation'. Available at: http://www.dlr.de/pa/desktopdefault. aspx/tabid-2349/3501_read-9919/ (accessed 20 December 2009).

Department of Transport, 2008. *Public Experiences of and Attitudes to Air Travel*. Office of National Statistics' omnibus survey. London: Transport Statistics..

Department of Transport, 2009. 'UK Statistics Report a Quadrupling of Passengers and Trebling of Emissions since 1980'24 February. Available at: http://www.greenaironline.com/news.php?viewStory=381 (accessed 24 February 2009).

Domain-b.com, 2008. 'British Airways Chief Criticises EU's Emission Trading Scheme'. 19 July. Available at: http://domain-b.com/aero/gov_reg/20080719_trading_scheme.html (accessed 15 November 2009).

Essenhigh, R., 2001. 'Does CO2 Really Drive Global Warming?' Available at: http://pubs.acs.org/subscribe/journals/ci/31/special/may01_viewpoint.html (accessed 5 November 2009).

European Union, 2005. 'Questions & Answers on Aviation & Climate Change'. Press release. 27 September. Available at: http://europa.eu/rapid/pressReleasesAction.do?reference=MEMO/05/341&format=HTML&aged=0&language=EN&guiLanguage=en (accessed 5 November 2009).

Fourier, J., 1826. *Annales de chimie et de Physique*. Paris: Crochard Libraire.

Gelsi, S., 2009. 'Exxon Mobil Lays $600 Million on the Line for Algae Fuels'. 14 July. Available at: http://www.marketwatch.com/story/exxon-mobil-lays-out-600-million-for-algae-fuels (accessed 14 July 2009).

Geocraft, 2003. 'Global Warming: A Closer Look at the Numbers'. Available at: http://www.geocraft.com/WVFossils/greenhouse_data.html (accessed 29 November 2009).

Google, 2009. 'Google's Green Initiatives'. Going Green at Google. Available at: http://www.google.com/corporate/green (accessed 4 November 2009).

Greener by Design, 2001. *Air Travel – Greener by Design: The Technology Challenge*. Conference Report of the Technology Sub-Group. Available at: http://www.greenerbydesign.org.uk/_FILES/publications/GbD%20-%202003%The%20Tech%20Challenge.pdf (accessed 9 June 2010).

Greenpeace, 2009. 'Pigs Take Flight as Airlines Claims They'll Cut Emissions by 50%'. 22 September. Available at: http://www.greenpeace.org.uk/blog/climate/pigs-take-flight-airlines-claim-theyll-cut-emissions-50-20090922 (accessed 22 September 2009).

Henderson, G., 2007. 'Livestock's Long Shadow?' 16 October. Available at: http://www.drovers.com/news_editorial.asp?pgid=717&ed_id=4354 (accessed 15 November 2009).

Hill, A., 2007. 'Travel: The New Tobacco'. *Observer*, 6 May.

Hundal, S., 2009. 'Stern: Climate Change Deniers are 'Flat-earthers'. 10 March. Available at: http://www.guardian.co.uk/environment/2009/mar/10/nicholas-stern-accuses-climate-change-deniers (accessed 10 March 2009).

ICAO, 2009. 'Aviation's Contribution to Climate Change'. Summary paper circulated at the High-level Meeting on International Aviation and Climate Change. Montreal, Canada 7–9 October.

ImpactLab, 2008. 'China's Big Airport Expansion Plan'. 27 January. Available at: http://www.impactlab.com/2008/01/27/chinas-big-airport-expansion-plan/ (accessed 20 September 2009).

IEA Statistics, 2009. *CO$_2$ Emissions from Fuel Combustion*. 2009 edition, 89–91. Paris: International Energy Agency.

Intergovernmental Panel on Climate Change (IPCC), 2007. 'Summary for Policy Makers'. In S. Solomon, D. Qin, M. Manning, Z. Chen, M. Marquis, K.B. Avery, M. Tignor and H.L. Miller (eds), *Climate Change 2007: The Physical Science Basis. Contribution of Working Group 1 to the Fourth Assessment Report of the Intergovernmental Panel on Climate Change*. Cambridge and New York: Cambridge University Press. Available at: http://www.ipcc.ch/pdf/assessment-report/ar4/wg1/ar4-wg1-spm.pdf (accessed 9 June 2010).

Intergovernmental Panel on Climate Change (IPCC), 2009. *Aviation and the Global Atmosphere. 7. Issues for the Future*. Available at: http://www.grida.no/publications/other.ipcc_sr/?src=/climate/ipcc/aviation/index.htm (accessed 9 June 2010).

Laumer, J., 2006. 'Evangelical Christian Leaders Urge Proactive Climate Solution'. 2 September. Available at: http://www.treehugger.com/files/2006/02/evangelical_chr.php (accessed 10 December 2009).

Leake, J., 2006. 'It's a Sin to Fly, Says Church'. 23 June Available at: http://www.timesonline.co.uk/tol/news/uk/article691423.ece (accessed 20 December 2009).

Leake, J. and Woods, R., 2009. 'Revealed: The Environmental Impact of Google Searches'. *The Sunday Times*, 11 January 2009.

Lycos Retriever, n.d. 'Svante Arrhenius'. Available at: http://www.lycos.com/info/svante-arrhenius.html (accessed 9 June 2010).

Lyons, L., 2005. 'One-Third of Americans Believe Dearly May Not Have Departed'. 12 July. Available at: http://www.gallup.com/poll/17275/onethird-americans-believe-dearly-may-departed.aspx (accessed 15 November 2009).

Mackenzie, K., 2009. 'BP Jatropha Venture: In Case You Were Wondering …'. 17 July. Available at: http://blogs.ft.com/energy-source/2009/07/17/bps-jatropha-venture-in-case-you-were-wondering/ (accessed 17 July 2009).

Maplecroft, 2009. 'Australia Overtakes USA as Top Polluter, Reveals Maplecroft CO$_2$ Emissions from Energy Index'. 9 September. Available at: http://maplecroft.com/news/australia_overtakes_usa_as_top_polluter_09.php (accessed 9 September 2009).

McGill University, 2009. Conference: Avoiding Dangerous Climate Change: Geo-engineering or Mitigation? The Lorne Trottier Public Science Symposium. Montreal: University of McGill, 19 November.

Moores, V., 2007. 'EasyJet Reveals Eco-friendly Aircraft Concept'. 14 June. Available at: http://www.flightglobal.com/articles/2007/06/14/214641/easyjet-reveals-eco-friendly-aircraft-concept.html (accessed 5 December 2009).

Murray, J., 2009. 'Scientists Claim First-generation Biofuels Here to Stay'. 12 March. Available at: http://www.businessgreen.com/business-green/news/2238371/agricultural-improvements-hold (accessed 12 March 2009).

O'Leary, M., 2006. 'O'Leary Gives Sermon to Bishop on Travel "Sins"'. *The Independent*, 27 July 2009.

Pew Research, 2009. 'Fewer Americans See Solid Evidence of Global Warming'. 22 October. Available at: http://pewresearch.org/pubs/1386/cap-and-trade-global-warming-opinion (accessed 18 November 2009).

Point Carbon, 2009. 'Airlines May Face €1bn Carbon Trading Cost from 2012'. 3 August. Available at: http://www.pointcarbon.com/aboutus/pressroom/pressreleases/1.1178592 (accessed 3 August 2009).

Raper, S. 2009. 'MAGAVIATION: Assessing the Potential Impact of Aviation Growth on Global Temperature Changes'. Available at: http://www.omega.mmu.ac.uk/Studies/MAGAVIATION.pdf (accessed 1 December 2009).

RenewableEnergyWorld, 2009. 'Boeing, Honeywell & Masdar Launch Study of Jet Fuel Made from Saltwater Plants'. 7 January. Available at: http://www.renewableenergyworld.com/rea/news/article/2009/10/boeing-honeywell-masdar-launch-study-of-jet-fuel-made-from-saltwater-plants (accessed 7 October 2009).

Reuters, 2009. 'Travel Agent Scraps "Medieval Pardons" for Emissions'. 16 October. Available at: http://blogs.reuters.com/environment/2009/10/16/travel-agent-scraps-medieval-pardons-for-emissions/ (accessed 16 October 2009).

Riddell, P. and Webster, B., 2009. 'Global Warming is not our Fault, Say Most Voters in Times Poll. *The Times,* 14 November 2009.

Singer, S.F., 2001. Letter to Editor. *Wall Street Journal*. 10 September.

Takahashi, J., 2009. 'Japanese Researchers Discover Method to Stop Cattle from Emitting Methane'. 31 March. Available at: http://www.agrometeorology.org/news/whats-new/japanese-researchers-discover-method-to-stop-cattle-from-emitting-methane (accessed 31 March 2009).

Times Online, 2008. 'Nuclear-powered Passenger Aircraft "to Transport Millions" Says Expert'. 27 October. Available at: http://www.timesonline.co.uk/tol/news/environment/article5024190.ece (accessed 15 December 2009).

Turner, A., 2009. 'Zero Emissions Aircraft Takes First Flight'. *Flight International*, 9 July.

Tyndall Centre for Climate Change Research, n.d. 'Who was John Tyndall?' Available at: http://www.tyndall.ac.uk/About/Who-was-John-Tyndall (accessed 4 October 2009).

Vaughan, A., 2009. 'British Public Refuse to Fly Less to Reduce their Carbon Footprint'. *Guardian*, 5 October. Available at: http://www.guardian.co.uk/environment/2009/oct/05/british-public-flights-carbon-footprint (accessed 26 May 2010).

Venter, C., 2008. '18 Months to 4th Generation Biofuels' (video). Available at: http://www.uncommondescent.com/biology/craig-venter-18-months-to-4th-generation-biofuels/ (accessed 2 February 2009).

Von Bulow, M., 2009. 'The Essentials of Copenhagen'. Available at: http://www. standardsusers.org/mysr/index.php?option=com_content&view=artic le&id=465:the-essentials-in-copenhagen&catid=73:articles&Itemid=83 (accessed 9 June 2010).

Wallace, J., 2002. 'Sonic Cruiser is Shelved'. 19 December. Available at: http://www.seattlepi.com/business/100543_sonic19.shtml (accessed 5 November 2009).

Walsh, W., 2008. Speech delivered at the Third Aviation & Environment Summit. Geneva, 22–23 April 2008. Available at: http://www.enviro. aero/Content/Upload/File/Willie%20Walsh%20speech.pdf (accessed 9 June 2010).

Webster, B., 2007. 'Ryanair Chief Flies into a Rage over Green Taunts'. *The Times*, 29 November 2007. Also available at: http://business.timesonline. co.uk/tol/business/industry_sectors/transport/article2963702.ece.

Whitelegg, J. and Williams, N., 2000. *The Plane Truth: Aviation and the Environment*. Transport 2000 Trust and the Ashden Trust. Available at: http://www.areco.org/planetr.pdf (accessed 26 May 2010).

Zakaria, F., 2008. 'A Bug to Save the Planet'. *Newsweek*, 16 June. Available at: http://www.newsweek.com/id/140066 (accessed 4 September 2009).

Chapter 8

'Here Comes the Sun': 20–20 Vision

Stormy Skies has focused on some key challenges facing airline management today and in the future. I will not pretend that all challenges have been addressed. Indeed, the choice of subjects is rather a personal one and you, the reader, may well feel as though I should have discussed others. The purpose of the book is to raise awareness and create debate on specific issues which, depending on airline management actions, might stave off some of the effects of an economic downturn. Some of these issues are under direct management control; others will be thrust upon management by external forces, whether they like it or not.

In order to broaden the discussion beyond my own opinions I asked a group of senior executives in the air transport business to come up with their 'top three' major issues, in order of priority, which the industry will need to address by 2020. Sometimes, the answers flowed instantaneously, and sometimes my contributor asked for time to reflect. All of them deserve thanks for their inputs and their cooperation.

My first contributor is Tony Tyler, Chief Executive Officer of Cathay Pacific Airways. Cathay Pacific, like many of the world's network carriers, was severely hit by the downturn. Indeed, the airline suffered more than many European carriers owing to their heavy reliance on premium traffic.

My next contributor is Tim Jeans, Chief Executive Officer of Monarch Airlines, a UK-based scheduled and charter operator. Tim describes 2009 as 'a year you'd rather forget'. Monarch Airlines was subject to rather different forces at work. For example, the airline's primary revenue source currency is sterling, which weakened substantially against both the dollar and the euro during the 2009 crisis, exacerbating the problems of weak demand.

Nico Buchholz spearheads the aircraft capacity strategy for Lufthansa, holding the position of Executive Vice President Corporate Fleet. Lufthansa was hit by reducing traffic volume in the crisis but was cushioned by a diversified business strategy, as the airline is present in many regions and serves different market segments. Also, Lufthansa's strategy of performing rapid reconfigurations of long-haul aircraft enabled it to adapt to changing market conditions at extremely short notice.

Air France is represented by Patrick Bianquis, Vice President Alliances. Like Lufthansa, Air France is a vigorous defender and supporter of consolidation. Patrick contends that consolidation will continue to the degree that, one day, between five and ten large global airlines will remain, in addition to regional and local carriers.

I also asked two senior executives from the major manufacturers to contribute their views on industry challenges for 2020. Boeing's Vice President Marketing, Randy Tinseth, and Airbus's Executive Vice President Head of Strategy and Future Programmes, Christian Scherer, both took a refreshingly broad view of the future. The manufacturers must wrestle with internal challenges of defining long-term product strategies as well as deal with the impact of the current crisis on their customers. And that is quite a juggling act.

My final contribution is from someone who can lay claim to being the happiest chief executive officer in the aviation industry today. Paul Griffiths is responsible for Dubai's international airport, as well as Al Maktoum International, a massive new airport and part of the Dubai World Central logistics and commercial development. Unlike most CEOs, Paul's challenge is how to deal with endless growth rather than declining passenger numbers.

Tony Tyler

1. Too much capacity
   'If you look back in history, the airline industry has always been plagued by too much capacity for the markets we are serving.'
2. Too much cost
   'Some are imposed by governments who see us as a licence to print tax money, or are imposed by governments that don't invest properly in infrastructure and therefore cause massive congestion.'
3. Weak markets
   'Partly due to excessive competition, there are 230 of us scrambling around to fill our planes and we're finding it very difficult.'

Tony Tyler is a firm believer in consolidation and is uncomfortable with the fact that the airline industry is so competitive: 'There are three big alliances all out to kill each other, so I don't take the point that consolidation is eliminating competition.'

Tim Jeans

1. Emissions trading
2. Fuel prices
   'The potential for fuel prices to go skyrocketing again as world economies recover is very great and that will impose significant cost pressures on our industry.'
3. Infrastructure
   'Air traffic, airports, congestion, and the costs of infrastructure development, which are getting somewhat out of hand.'

Tim Jeans has the United Kingdom very much in mind when he speaks of congestion. He believes that passenger convenience will drive the decision to fly or take the train in Britain: 'People will default to surface transport because we've collectively made the air product so inconvenient for people to use on short journeys, particularly with security.'

Nico Buchholz

1. Infrastructure
   'The availability of space and slots will become more severe.'
2. Noise
3. Efficiency versus choice.

   Nico Buchholz believes that the industry must find a solution to the conundrum of how much choice it is willing to offer to the market in terms of frequencies, against driving efficiency by forcing the market into larger, more efficient, but less frequent flights.

Patrick Bianquis

1. Fuel and emissions trading
2. Business model competition
   Patrick's point is that in Europe the business market will be provided with a choice between rail travel and using the low-cost carriers.
3. Economics
   'We've never been profitable and we don't know exactly why! The margin of potential profitability is passed directly to the consumer and that doesn't happen in other industries.'

Randy Tinseth

1. The environment
   'That's going to be a huge issue at that time (2020). The future is going to be about new efficient airplanes, improvements in air traffic management, as well as bringing biofuels to the market.'
2. Finding the right product strategy
   Here, Randy is thinking about how the manufacturer can meet the requirements of its customers. 'I've been to so many markets where low-cost carriers had no market share ten years ago, and today they supply 40 per cent or 50 per cent of seats. You have to make sure you have to have the right strategy that's aligned

to the realities of the marketplace.'
3. Remaining competitive
'We have long-lived assets, and we have a market that changes. How do you use these assets and change at the same time?'

Randy also added a fourth and fifth item to his list, being infrastructure and the environment.

Christian Scherer

1. Air Traffic Management
'The hassle associated with delays and flight cancellations can be significantly reduced if we all pull together – legislators, airlines, manufacturers, avionics suppliers – and we produce, collectively, an efficient air traffic management system that avoids congestion and optimises flight paths.' Christian believes that an optimised system could yield up to 10 per cent fuel savings.
2. The environment
'The travelling public and political circles need to understand how much air transportation is a GDP driver and not a polluter. Protesting isn't the right way to do it. Education is a better way.'
3. Security and safety
'The safety record is extremely high, but it is a significant challenge to maintain this level of integrity. Safety has got to remain the top, top, top challenge.'

Paul Griffiths

1. Sustainability
'We've got to find an alternative fuel source and it can only be solved by new technology. We need to build sustainable aircraft but accept that this might still be seen as a bit despicable in some people's eyes.' Paul is intimating that, despite our best efforts to minimise environmental impact, aviation just has to get used to criticism. That's life.

2. Our ability to build capacity

'We are living in an age where the link between prosperity and gross domestic product growth is not seen as positive. On the contrary, an airport development is often seen as a blight on the landscape.' Of course, the powerhouse of Dubai, and the growth of Emirates in particular, depends utterly on a continuous flow of airport capacity. 'Nothing can stand in the way of capacity development. We shall not flinch,' says Paul Griffiths. Such determination and confidence reinforces the notion that Dubai will ultimately become the crossroads of the world, easily accessible from every major industrial region. Indeed, Paul dismisses the danger of overcapacity: 'Capacity is relative to the market, and our market is the world. Emirates is stealing a few points of market share from every airline it competes with on the planet and is consequently able to spread risk.'

3. Potential disappearance of the low-cost model

Paul Griffiths asks, 'How long will the low-cost phenomenon last?' He believes it will depend on his previous two predictions. 'If you can't add capacity, you spill demand and the price will go up. It's an economic challenge. Air travel will not continue to be as cheap as it is now.' He is convinced that in the future there will be no discernible difference between low-cost and full service operators.

And Finally…

I cannot resist offering my own 'top three' challenges for the airline industry in 2020.

1. The environment

This issue will still be a top agenda item for governments and lobbyists in 2020. Although it is principally the wealthier nations stepping up to the mark in 2010, environmental responsibility is likely to permeate every action we take and involve all nations. Identifying acceptable practices and solutions to mitigate environmental impact will be a particularly tough challenge for our industry, but our track record of innovation stands us in good stead. Whether there will be global agreement on emissions standards by 2020 is less certain. I predict that the question on whether global warming is really due to carbon emissions or not will still be a matter for hot debate. It may be that we will have found another issue to worry about by 2020. I suspect that once we become more confident that solutions can be found, such as renewable energy sources and carbon neutral activities, then global attention might switch to another hazard. Indeed, history shows that our attention span, even on matters of global importance, is finite. Next on the environmentalists' list could be a global water shortage. Who knows?

2. Stronger focus on the passenger

   Within the next ten years global economies will have recovered, and it can be expected that airlines will experience another traditional boom before the next traditional bust. Air travel will have become increasingly commoditised except for niche and very long-haul operations, airports will be struggling to cope with demand, and delays will become longer. But there is a limit to what passengers will put up with. I predict a backlash from ordinary travellers, who will galvanise widespread support through the power of social media. The tide will be turning by 2020, and providers of capacity and operators of aircraft will be introducing strategies to radically improve the conditions under which people travel. Regulators will step in to set standards and enforce them. Such standards will cover areas such as airport processing procedures and minimum personal space per passenger on aircraft.

3. The aircraft and airport interface

   By 2020 we may be seriously evaluating a long-awaited overhaul of the interface between aircraft and airport, with a more flexible approach to airport terminal design, and a rethink of the time-honoured but archaic practice of separating passengers from their baggage, processing two separate streams of payload, carrying them separately, then reuniting them all again at the end of every journey flown. It is expensive, unreliable and prone to failure. This system may have suited the age of transatlantic luxury liners a century ago, when the rich and famous expected others to take care of their luggage, but it is hardly appropriate for the mass travel market of the twenty-first century. The rail industry solved this problem; now it's the airline industry's turn.

It will not be resolved by 2020, but pressures on the air transport system are likely to act as a catalyst for a fresh look at the whole issue.

Of course, all it takes is for one Black Swan to swoop down upon us, and we may have to go back to the drawing board. But, at least for the moment, here comes the sun!

Index

Figures are indicated by **bold** page numbers.